# LEARNING MATTERS
## The truth about our schools

by Roger Titcombe

ISBN-10: 149921300X
ISBN-13: 9781499213003

## DEDICATION

To my wife Karen for her support.

## ACKNOWLEDGMENTS

I am grateful to the following distinguished academics for correspondence and comments on my manuscript:

Philip Adey

Michael Shayer

Peter Saunders

Clive Sutton of Leicester University School of Education for teaching and inspiring me about theories of learning.

The Learning Trust and Hackney Learning Trust for reading, commenting and correcting Part 4 of my manuscript.

All of the huge number of skilled and dedicated teachers at every level in the schools in which I have served that have worked alongside me and shared their expertise, giving me good advice and support in my teaching career since 1971.

Especially my publisher, English teacher and author Francis Gilbert for our many challenging and insightful discussions about the manuscript from his perspective as a non-scientist.

# Contents

## *If you read only one book on education, read this one...*

It is my firm belief this passionate polemic is one of the most important investigations into education published in the last twenty years. Why? There are two reasons:

First, Roger Titcombe really shows you more clearly than anyone else where things have gone wrong in schools.

Second, he offers genuine, practical solutions to the problems.

This is a book both about the tragedy of millions of lives scarred by educational failure, but it also offers genuine hope: it is both a rigorously researched polemic and a guide.

There are a number of things that make Roger Titcombe's polemical guide so unique. It is written by a teacher but it is not exclusively *for* teachers, although, I am sure, many will find it essential reading. It combines gritty, no-nonsense analysis with powerful personal stories that show beyond doubt that a toxic cocktail of factors have poisoned our school system.

There have been many books which have outlined the problems of our system but very few have brought together so many disparate elements into a coherent whole: Titcombe's scope is huge. He not only analyses our school system, but he shows us how children learn, how we think, how free markets work, how marketised education is linked to social disorder and how successive governments have implemented policies that have stopped learning happening in our schools.

It's worth here going through Titcombe's central arguments because once you've got the "big picture" of what he's saying, you'll better appreciate the masterful way he marshals his arguments and evidence.

Throughout the book Titcombe illustrates with a number of powerful examples why our examination system, school league tables and competition between schools since the late 1980s has caused a catastrophic change in the way our pupils are taught. Put bluntly, our schools are making students stupider. This isn't primarily our teachers' fault but the fault of a system which encourages students to learn in a very superficial fashion. Instead of learning deeply, students are drilled to pass exams and pretty much forget everything they've learnt after they've taken them.

What is exceptional about this book is the evidence Titcombe provides to back up his points. This is no woolly liberal diatribe against exams-per-se because Titcombe argues if used sensibly exams can be a powerful tool for helping students learn in a "deep fashion". Throughout the book, Titcombe refers to Cognitive Ability Tests or CATs for short (a form of IQ test widely used for school admissions) because they are the most reliable measure we have of students' current cognitive ability levels. You don't have to be a fully paid-up believer in IQ tests to agree with Titcombe's points. Personally, I think IQ tests are not always a reliable test of intelligence in individual cases but the general picture they paint is tremendously powerful: they are a much more reliable indicator of the state of intellectual development of a pupil than most external exams, like the SATs tests administered in the UK at the moment. Most serious educationalists would accept Titcombe's diagnosis: we have a school system at the moment that is very poor at getting children to master the challenging concepts needed to become more intelligent. Titcombe believes that intelligence is plastic: it can be increased or inhibited by the nature of schooling. Sadly, we have the worst of both worlds. We have students who pass their exams with flying colours and think they're really clever (when they're not) and a lot of students who have failed their exams and think they're really stupid (when they're not). Read this book, and learn just how inane our current exam system is: it makes for damning, chilling reading.

Many commentators – both on the left and right -- have said similar things to this but not many (none I would dare to say) have joined the dots in the way that Titcombe has: *Learning Matters* is superb at tying together many disparate threads. Titcombe manages to show that the shift from a locally accountable school system to one which is both very centralised and market-driven has meant that many schools have chucked "deep learning" out of the window in favour of "quick fixes" to get good exam results. He points out how all of us have been affected by this change: the way we're taught has wrought an insidious, hidden change in the way we relate to each other as human beings. We have become a society which not only has a social underclass but a "cognitive" one as well. This has made us more dependent in our lives on consumerism, achieving status through spending our money on things instead of relating to each other in meaningful ways.

This is a very brave book because it will alienate people both on the left and right. Many people on the left may have serious problems with the way Titcombe suggests that poorer communities have become dumber, while those on the right won't like his eviscerating attack on the way a market-driven school system has eroded educational standards. It is a fearless book: Titcombe goes where no serious educational commentator has dared to tread.

Read it and weep, but also note its message of hope. Titcombe shows that it wouldn't take that much to change things. He welcomes some of the changes recent government has made to the examination system but says that they need to go further. He points out that every teacher could defy the current predilection for superficial learning and modify their practice to teach "deep learning". I know I've changed the way I teach as a result of reading this book.

By Francis Gilbert

## *Foreword*

The format of this book is deliberately unusual. I hope it will be read by educationalists, teachers, academics, students and politicians, but also by parents and the general public.

It is in part academic educational research, part political polemic and part personal recollections and anecdotes. These genres are normally kept well apart, so I am breaking the rules. If you are reading the e-book version you will find embedded links to the relevant references that are freely available on-line. If you are reading the paper version then these links are <u>underlined</u>.

The recollections and anecdotes are provided in a parallel commentary. They are intended to provide contact points with normal life - groundings, as relief from the heavier stuff, as well as being an insight into where I have come from in writing this book, which I have been doing on and off since 2003, when I retired from the headship of an inner urban secondary school in an industrial northern town.

My personal political perspective will be fairly clear, which may well result in those of a different view rejecting my book without reading further. I hope not: the academic core of my book is relevant to everybody with an interest in education.

I owe a lot to the internet forum, <u>Local Schools Network (LSN)</u>, to which I am a regular contributor. LSN has become very influential, with thousands of hits per week. It has a management committee comprising a mixture of political commentators, authors, journalists, educational researchers, school governors and retired teachers. Some wear more than one hat quite comfortably. They are all broadly on the political left, but by no means uniformly so. However, LSN is open to all that wish to contribute and comment and attracts posts from the whole of the political spectrum and all sections of the education debate.

Many extracts from this book have been previously posted on LSN and the resulting feedback, supportive and deeply critical alike, have helped me to refine the text. Many of the parallel commentaries have also appeared on LSN. Where there is no named author then it is my work. In other cases the name of the author is given and I am grateful to them for permission to include their work.

I am relentlessly critical of the post 1988 Education Reform Act English school system and this includes what has been happening in many individual schools. However, with one exception, I have not commented on any named school. This is quite deliberate. The first reason is that schools change and any comments may become quickly out of date. The second reason is that schools are precious to pupils and parents and in all cases teachers work hard and do their best. I believe I have been able to make the necessary points strongly enough without naming individual schools.

The exception is Mossbourne Community Academy in Hackney. The reason is that I am holding this school up as an example of the power of a comprehensive school to transform the life chances of pupils from all social and ethnic backgrounds. In my view it points to the best way forward for urban schooling, with many lessons for comprehensive schools and systems in every part of the country. I also commend the work of The Learning Trust (a private not-for-profit company) and the Hackney Learning Trust (part of Hackney Borough Council) into which it has been transformed. I come to these conclusions as a result of my study of Mossbourne, which is set out in Part Four.

My book argues that there is an urgent need for a fundamental change in the direction, governance and public accountability of the English education system. In writing it I have become aware that this is a view that is widely shared by education professionals, teachers and increasingly parents, but it has not been at all reflected in the mainstream media.

I have done my utmost to make sure that my book is free from errors. If you find any factual errors, please contact me through my publisher: sir@francisgilbert.co.uk. Significant errors can be corrected.

If my book contributes in even the smallest way by clarifying what is meant by 'good education' and in bringing about the necessary changes, I will be very happy.

## Part 1

*What has gone wrong and*
*how did we get here?*

## 1.1 The paradox between improved exam results and degraded education

This book is about the state of the English education system in the second decade of the 21st century.

We can make a start with the mismatch between the ever-rising GCSE results of English pupils and their schools and the common media and public perception that educational standards are falling. This perception is reinforced by the comparatively poor performance of the English system in the international comparisons carried out through the Organisation for Economic Co-operation and Development's (OECD) Programme for International Student Assessment (PISA) system.

In 2005, in partnership with Roger Davies, a professional statistician, I carried out research into the common features of the 'most improved' schools as reported in the annual school performance tables. This work was sponsored by *TES* and featured in January 2006. The full report was published on the *TES* website. We found a common pattern in which school improvement in performance table terms was linked to an impoverished curriculum that limited rather than enhanced the life chances of pupils. This is an extraordinary claim that requires appropriate evidence. This is set out in Part 3.

The research is detailed and not available elsewhere. For example, the common but mistaken view is that schools' exam results are openly published by the government in the form of the annual performance tables with a mountain of further information available from the Department for Education (DfE) website. Despite changes in the Performance Tables the really important information, the detailed subject by subject record of numbers of pupils entered and grades achieved, is still not readily available and can only be obtained if you know what you are looking for and what questions to ask.

The second vital area where there is much confusion is school admissions arrangements. This has become the most important issue for securing the future of schools in the league table era, for many complex reasons that are rarely understood by most parents and the media. This issue is addressed in the Part 4 case study.

Mossbourne Community Academy has for a long time been the media's favourite example of how the Academies programme, introduced by Labour Prime Minister Tony Blair, appeared to be successfully overcoming the long-standing comparatively low GCSE performance of schools serving economically and socially deprived communities. The 2013 School Performance Tables referred to this process as, 'Closing the Gap'.

This book questions the nature of this 'gap'. According to a *Guardian* article on 23 January 2011, the Mossbourne pupils' success prompted John Bald, a former head inspector at OfSTED, to describe it as "a spectacular breakthrough". He called Mossbourne "the best comprehensive in the country". In January 2012 the Executive Principal of Mossbourne, Sir Michael Wilshaw, was appointed Chief Inspector of Schools (Head of OfSTED), presumably in recognition of this achievement. The reasons that underpin the success of Mossbourne Academy are explored in Part 4.

This book persistently and repeatedly reveals the misleading nature of the presentation of education policies of successive governments from Thatcher to Cameron, that has largely been accepted at face value by an uncritical media. The truth is frequently both surprising and counter intuitive. Revealing this truth is often parodied as justifying under-performance, when the opposite is the case.

## C 1.1 Origins and Perspectives

*I was born in 1947, the only child of working class parents. My father was 'respectable' working class, my mother possibly less so. My father's mother died in childbirth having him and his father remarried. Astonishingly, he didn't find out about this and that his mother was really his step-mum until late in life. His dad had been an ambulance driver in World War I and before that had been something of an adventurer in Canada. In World War II he was a fireman. One night putting out fires during the Birmingham blitz, he fell from a ladder and was badly injured.*

*My grandmother on my mother's side was Irish, born into a large family in Queens County (now County Offaly) in 1897. Her father was murdered in front of the family by an IRA assassin in 1921. So far as we can gather his 'crime' was to be a postman, therefore working for the government of the enemy. There were a number of such murders around that time.*

*She left her family in Ireland and sailed to Liverpool with her sister, moving on to Birmingham. Her sister settled in Tipton in the Black Country. My grandmother married a market stall holder, a hard drinking Brummie from Kings Heath who ill-treated her and her two daughters until he died in 1952. That turned out to be a significant event in my family's lives.*

*In 1936 at the age of 15 my father was apprenticed to the engineering firm, John Ackworthie Ltd, of Coleshill Street, Birmingham until his 21st birthday. His trade was 'toolmaker' and for a standard working week of 47 hours his starting pay was 10 shillings (50p) per week on a guaranteed rising scale over a 7 year period. Overtime was paid at double the ordinary rate. (How much progress has been made in the employment of school leavers since then?). During World War II, engineering was a 'reserved' occupation and he met my mother in an armaments factory. This was not a match that his step-mother approved of, since my mother's family was definitely not 'respectable working class'.*

*After the war they married and had me. However, they were homeless without a place to live with either parents, so they bought a tiny caravan and had it towed to a site in Wooton Wawen, near Henley-in-Arden, about 20 miles south of Birmingham. However this arrangement did not last for reasons that I don't know, so my very early years were spent living in a field up 'Brickyard Hill' where the caravan was pitched by an old well which provided our water supply. My father worked for an engineering firm he called, 'The Maudslay', near Alcester to which he cycled every day. My Irish grandmother visited us by bus from Birmingham from time to time. She adored me and I her.*

*In 1950 my mother somehow managed to get me enrolled at the age of three into the local school. It was housed in a tiny Victorian hall on the left side of the A34, on the hill up to Henley-in-Arden from Wooton Wawen. I remember my first day at school (I cried) and the smell of plasticine.*

## 1.2 What are schools for?

We have become used to accepting the idea that the quality of a school is measured by the degree of year-on-year improvement in raw exam results and that learning processes such as playing with plasticine are at best irrelevant and at worst a barrier to the acquisition of knowledge.

This book argues the case for a developmental approach to education. It is based on the idea that *attainment,* in all its forms and contexts, is founded on general *abilities* and that it is the job of schools to recognise and to promote the development of these underlying abilities. At the same time a school should be maximising students' attainment in their academic studies and nurturing the physical, artistic and social skills that grow out of these talents and abilities. My book draws heavily on the work and ideas of Jean Piaget and Lev Vygotsky.

Much of what follows is based on the concept of general intelligence and the validity of its routine measurement by means of commercially available Cognitive Ability Tests (CATs).

Although the basis for the routine work of Educational Psychologists for more than half a century and the current CATs based admissions systems for hundreds of state funded schools since the inception of the Academies programme, the general intelligence factor 'g' is a concept about which much heat has been generated.

Many left inclined educationalists still begin any discussion in this area with an IQ denial statement of some form. I am happy just to accept the fact that cognitive ability, regardless of arguments about its philosophical significance, can be readily measured by relatively simple, albeit increasingly sophisticated, tests and that their results have very high correlations with life outcomes and especially with performance in the education system.

Are there other sorts of intelligence? We certainly don't all think the same way, which is why standardised cognitive ability tests have three sub-test components: verbal, quantitative and non-verbal. Although most individuals score similarly on each component, some do not, revealing differences in cognitive strategies and abilities in the three areas.

Howard Gardner went much further with his theory of multiple intelligences (1983), which is an attractive, popular and frequently quoted rebuttal of the concept of general intelligence. Gardner proposes seven distinct and independent 'intelligences' with two, 'linguistic intelligence' and 'logical-mathematical intelligence' roughly corresponding with the qualities measured by Cognitive Ability Tests (CATs). The other five, although claimed to be independent by Gardner, in fact correlate to a greater or lesser degree with the first two. To the extent that they correlate highly, they are more clearly understood as components of 'g'. Those that correlate more weakly seem to be more like 'talents' further examples of the rich diversity of human variation to be encouraged and celebrated, but not so strongly predictive of general exam performance and broader life outcomes.

Chapter 12 of 'Bad Education - Debunking Myths in Education' (2012) edited by Philip Adey and Justin Dillon, addresses the myths of both 'intelligence fixed at birth' and 'multiple intelligences'.

The arguments in this book are based on the validity of general intelligence as set out by Adey and others but with the insistence that although resilient, such general intelligence is plastic and that its development should be the priority of all good schooling. 'Plasticity' is a precise engineering term relating to properties of materials. A 'plastic' material is one that can be permanently deformed (shape altered) by the application of an external stress. The opposites are 'brittle' (cracks under stress) and 'tough/resilient' (does not break under stress or permanently deform - may spring back). In this book 'plastic intelligence' means that cognitive ability and level of cognitive sophistication can be permanently changed through perception/experience combined with the right sort of teaching/learning.

'Plastic' general intelligence is a significantly different concept to 'fixed intelligence conferred at birth'. It opens the door to the development of the intellect of all children (and indeed adults) through good quality education. However much education practice commonly believed to be 'good' is in fact 'bad' and does not result in cognitive growth. That is a theme that runs throughout the book.

Steven Pinker, Professor of Psychology at Harvard University wrote in his book, *The Blank Slate* (p. 149, Pinker, 2002):

> I find it surreal to find academics denying the existence of intelligence. Academics are obsessed with intelligence. They discuss it endlessly in considering student admissions, in hiring faculty and staff, and especially in their gossip about one another. Nor can citizens or policy makers ignore the concept, regardless of their politics. People who say IQ is meaningless will quickly invoke it when the discussion turns to the execution of a murderer with an IQ of 64, removing lead paint that lowers a child's IQ by 5 points, or the presidential qualifications of George W. Bush.

The academic arguments of the IQ deniers come down to the complex statistics of multi-variable correlations called factor analysis. These are the grounds on which Steven Jay Gould attempted to discredit 'general intelligence' in his much quoted 1981 book, *The Mismeasure of Man*.

For those that are interested in further exploration of these arguments I recommend the 'Afterword' by Charles Murray in the *The Bell Curve* (R.J. Herrnstein, C. Murray, 1994). This book gained notoriety mainly for a section on racial and ethnic variations in IQ. While I disagree with the authors about the plasticity of cognitive ability, which they seriously underrate, I judge their book to be a work of great scholarship and moderation on the question of general intelligence. It is unjustifiably reviled by many on the left of politics.

In our modern society, with its rich literary, scientific and technological culture, proficiency in manipulating complex information and problem solving within this culture correlates strongly with putting food on the table, a roof over the head and maximising any surplus wealth that can be acquired. Hunter-gatherer societies clearly produce different correlations. Value judgments about the qualities needed to prosper in different cultures that so obsess sociologists seem to me to be increasingly pointless as global capitalism spreads, promoting increasingly commonly shared concepts of meritocracy and opportunity founded in the modern commercial and industrial world.

There is no dispute that scores on cognitive ability tests correlate strongly with exam results and future life outcomes in our society and culture. This book is about recognising the plastic nature of intelligence and the opportunity it creates for enriching the lives of individuals and the quality of society through the promotion of cognitive development through national education systems.

The fact that a minority of individuals can exploit diverse talents in commercialised sport, the entertainment industries and the cult of celebrity, that are not directly related to cognitive ability, in no way invalidates this central truth about the value of quality schooling.

## C 1.2 My own schooling

In 1952 at the age of 5 I started at Wheeler's Lane Infant and Junior school in Birmingham. We lived close to the school gate. I was quick to learn at school and found myself in the 11 plus exam stream by Y5. Parents could list their preferred three selective schools in order of preference. My first choice was a long established grammar school in very old buildings. The second choice was a brand new 'Boys' Technical School. At first, I was allocated the Technical School, but later we received a letter saying I could have my first choice of the grammar school after all. By then we had visited the brand new well equipped Technical School, so my parents stuck with that. I suspect that the notion of newness and technical modernity trumped the classical associations of the grammar school for my working class parents.

In 1958, boy's secondary schools were brutal. Most teachers informally and routinely administered corporal punishment. A favourite of the PE teacher was to start gym lessons by making us hang from the top wall bar until the fat boy of the form became exhausted and was the first to fall to the floor. We all then dropped down together in relief, the fat boy being further humiliated by the jeers of the class.

*It is now clear to me that the culture of the school was for teachers to be in constant fear of chaos and insurrection on the part of their charges. To prevent any possibility of this the first rule of teaching was to inspire fear in the pupils. This was how boys' secondary schools usually worked at that time.*

*However, there were some very good teachers that made a big impression on me. One such was an elderly maths teacher, a kindly man who was a World War 1 veteran. He was one of the few teachers who never threatened us, hit us or threw the heavy blackboard duster at us. He told us things about his experience of the Great War that I did not understand at the time but which I remember to this day. He was also a keen bee-keeper and explained to us about the 'waggle dance' of bees that communicate directions to sources of nectar. The class was fascinated. This was about the time that this bee behaviour was first discovered. I joined the after-school 'Bee Club'. He also communicated to us Brummies his love for the Lake District and how he remembered Ullswater freezing over one Easter and people skating. My guess is that this must have been in 1947, the year of my birth. I became a keen fell walker and climber when at university. In 1969 I took part in a two-month overland university mountaineering expedition to the remote 'Pontic Alps' in North-east Turkey. This was near where American missiles were sited, which led to the 1962 Cuban missile crisis. We have lived on the edge of the Lake District National Park since 1989.*

## 1.3 A digression on human variation and equality

I have come to realise that my elderly maths teacher was an expert in developing and nurturing intelligence in many different ways. Many are uncomfortable with the concept of intelligence because of confusion between the fact of individual diversity and the commitment many of us share to equality. It is indisputable that individual humans, like all complex living species, vary in limitless ways in accordance with the Bell Curve Normal Distribution that has a precise mathematical description. This does not, however, confirm nor refute the principle of social and legal equality, which is a shared political assertion located in human minds, rather than an experimental, factual truth of the material world.

The most famous and probably most powerful historical declaration of the principle of universal human equality is that which underpins the constitution of the United States of America and which is generally attributed to Thomas Jefferson:

We hold these truths to be self-evident, that all men are created equal, that they are endowed by their Creator with certain

inalienable Rights, that among these are Life, Liberty, and the
Pursuit of Happiness. That to secure these rights, Governments
are instituted among Men, deriving their just powers from the
consent of the governed. (Jefferson, 1787)

This famous declaration has the wisdom and power to capture and
retain allegiance to what has become a universal principle across the
political and religious spectrum inspiring those of a secular as well
as many (but not all) of those of a religious disposition.

It is not necessary for the physical manifestations of individual
humans, either in part or as a whole, to be equal, as it is obvious that
they are not. Individuals may be shorter, fatter, uglier, less athletic,
less musical, less intelligent and less good at some or all sports.
Also, contrary to the usual primary school sugary version of
Christianity, Gods do not dispense their 'gifts' evenly or fairly. Some
people get an unremittingly poor hand, with either God or genetics
conspicuously failing to offset disadvantageous characteristics with
compensating gifts. When a beautiful actress proposed to George
Bernard Shaw with the argument, "imagine our children with your
brains and my beauty", he is said to have replied, "But what if they
got your brains and my beauty?"

Humans are equal in a different and more important way. They
have equal rights, such rights being broadly accepted throughout the
post-enlightenment world, which we have to hope still includes the
UK.

This is a simple confusion that those on the political right often
fail to understand. This famously includes Margaret Thatcher. On
this question she set out her stall in a speech of 16 September 1975
to Pilgrims of the United States ("Heritage and Horizon") in the
USA just a few months after she had been elected leader of the
Conservative Party.

> "The pursuit of equality itself is a mirage," she said. "Opportunity
> means nothing unless it includes the right to be unequal and the
> freedom to be different. One of the reasons why we value
> individuals is not because they're all the same but because they're
> all different ... Let our children grow tall and some taller than
> others, if they have the ability in them to do so."

The traditional standpoint of the political left is that the fruits of
the exploitation of such ability, however energetic or single minded,
cannot be allowed to impinge upon or limit the rights of the less
fortunate. The dim, the ugly and even the lazy all have equal rights
to the basic requirements for human happiness, including access to
decent housing, high quality education and healthcare, equal

treatment before the law, and protection from crime, corruption and exploitation.

My parents' generation, born in the early 1920s, desperately wanted, more than anything else, for their children to be better off than they were, having lived through the Great Depression and World War II. I want my children and grandchildren to continue to benefit from the equalising entitlements of the Welfare State bequeathed to us through the sacrifice and suffering of my parents' generation, like free access to high quality education and healthcare, the provision of decent affordable housing and security in old age. All of these are now threatened by the 2008 economic crisis and the resulting austerity that capitalist economics appears to prescribe for its solution. So although some on the political left may not like some of the rational arguments set out in this book, the author regards them as firmly rooted in the tradition of British democratic socialism.

I was born in 1947 and no generation has benefitted from a more favourable social legacy.

The current economic crisis and its imposition of austerity, contrasted with the escalating gross rewards of the ultra-rich, have brought equality and meritocracy firmly back onto the political agenda. These concepts have been researched, aired and debated by Will Hutton, Observer columnist and Chair of the Big Innovation Centre at 'The Work Foundation', who is now Principal of Hertford College, Oxford. While accepting the need for rewards linked to talent and hard work (meritocracy), in his 2011 book, *Them and Us: Changing Britain – Why we need a Fair Society*, Hutton calls for limits on the multiplier between the lowest and highest paid in every employing organisation, even when very high rewards can be justified by the profits earned for the company (as in the case of financial commodity traders) or the alleged need to compete for the best skilled managers and executives in a global market.

This contrasts with the position of Peter Saunders, Emeritus Professor of Sociology at Sussex University, whose reports *Social Mobility Myths* (2010) and *Social Mobility Delusions* (2012) argue for unbridled meritocracy. Saunders attacks what he calls the 'SAD' thesis - Social Advantage and Disadvantage conferred at birth through social class. In the 2010 book he says:

> "Back in the 1990s, I organised a survey in which a sample of the British population was asked to respond to three different statements about the 'fairest' way to establish individual entitlement to material resources.
>
> One of these statements represented the egalitarian ideal that

'people's incomes should be made more equal by taxing higher earners'. Just over half of the sample agreed with this while around one - third disagreed.

A second statement expressed the free market, libertarian position that 'people's incomes should depend on market demand for their services'. Again, something more than a half of respondents agreed and around one - third disagreed.

The final statement reflected the meritocratic ideal that 'people's incomes should depend on hard work and ability'. Fully 90 per cent of respondents agreed with this with fewer than 10 per cent disagreeing.

Few moral principles can command universal assent in a modern, pluralistic, individualistic society, but meritocracy clearly comes pretty close.

This strong support for meritocracy relative to the other two positions suggests that most of us understand that inequality is not in itself 'unfair'—it depends on whether it results from the application of individual talent and effort. If we are convinced that, by and large those who have the ability and who make an effort can usually gain success, then the basis is laid for a society which can function reasonably harmoniously. Meritocracy does have a problem dealing with the social consequences of failure, but this need not undermine social cohesion provided the competition is known to have been fair. Ninety per cent agreement is not a bad basis on which to build and sustain a moral social order."

As Professor Saunders is well aware, to be valid, questionnaires need to be very carefully constructed with the respondents allowed to qualify their responses. I maintain that if the words, "up to a point" had been included in the third proposition then the agreement rate would have been not 90 but 100 per cent. Since the same population was asked all three questions it seems obvious that the considerable support for propositions 1 and 2 shows that all three propositions can be happily supported at the same time if "up to a point" is included in all of them.

Human variation is a fact. Fairness doesn't come into it. However we humans have the power to incorporate our own articulation of fairness in the way we choose to organise democratic societies. This is the challenge that Thomas Jefferson and the 'founding fathers' rose to so magnificently. Meritocracy is fine and positive so long as the acquisitiveness of the clever, strong and talented does not compromise the rights of those at the other end of the Bell Curve of human variation. Harold Wilson went further in 1964 and I still agree with him. I want a firmly regulated meritocracy mediated by a welfare state paid for by progressive taxation, and see no reason to change this viewpoint just because the rich and powerful have become so very rich and so very powerful.

### C 1.3 My first political experience

*In 1964, at the age of 17, I attended my first public political event. It was a rally led by Harold Wilson campaigning for the General Election at Birmingham Rag Market before a huge crowd with no tickets or visible security of any kind. Wilson addressed the equality issue directly by invoking an image of a horse-drawn coach stuck in mud. "Who amongst the passengers should be the first to get down into the mud and push?" he asked. The answer of course was, "the strongest not the holders of the cheapest tickets". This might seem trite and simplistic to the cynical twenty-first century adult, but it had a profound effect on an idealistic teenager. I was reminded of Harold Wilson's speech by the centenary of the sinking of the Titanic in 1912. Those holding the cheapest tickets of this White Star Line ship were exceptionally poorly represented amongst the survivors.*

## 1.4 'Plastic Intelligence'

Harold Wilson and other socialists at that time believed that the advantages of a grammar school education could be shared with all children by extending the selective school model down the ability range. This envisaged a comprehensive school as being like a grammar school but with lots more streams. The fact that this didn't work led many on the left to assume that the barriers to success for less able children were rooted in class and social prejudice rather than in bad lessons. Mossbourne Community Academy is the modern example that shows that, unlike in the 11 plus system, this need not be the case in an all-ability comprehensive school (4.13). In other words the solution to the problem of working class children being trapped by poor education lies not in grammar school selection but in quality all-ability comprehensive provision.

Saunders is therefore largely correct in his analysis of the general fallacy of what he calls the SAD conspiracy thesis (1.3) by which he means the argument frequently made from the political left that social advantage and disadvantage is conferred at birth and keeps people within their social class stations regardless of ability and hard work:

> The SAD thesis is directly opposed to the meritocracy thesis, which suggests that even children born into the humblest of circumstances can succeed if they are bright and they work hard.

> The left wing sociological establishment regards any suggestion that occupational selection in Britain might be taking place on broadly meritocratic principles as literally incredible. The SAD thesis is their 'dominant paradigm' through which all evidence gets filtered, and against which all arguments are evaluated.

Saunders is correct in identifying the denial of the role of cognitive ability in accounting for the variation in exam outcomes of individuals and schools as a major cause of the misdirection and consequent failure of education policy.

I have tried to deal with what I call the Cognitive Ability Denial Fallacy but this does not mean that that individual cognitive ability need be fixed at birth or any subsequent age and still less that children and adults cannot significantly mediate the consequences of their genetic inheritance. While the SAD social science establishment usually denies any role for genetic inheritance of intelligence (or they would say the illusion of intelligence), there is virtually no-one that denies that environment, and that must include curriculum and schooling, can result in at least some acquired intelligence. While acquired intelligence may not be directly passed from parent to child through genes it can accrue in society as a whole through better nutrition, decent housing, better parenting and more powerfully still in my view by better schooling. In this context 'better' means qualitatively specific approaches to teaching and learning. While the relative contributions of possible environmental and cultural factors is fiercely debated, usually generating much more heat than light, growth in societal IQ for non-genetic reasons has been measured and is not in doubt.

This was acknowledged by Herrnstein and Murray in *The Bell Curve* and these authors first coined the name, 'The Flynn Effect' for this phenomenon first described by James Flynn in his studies (1987) of large rises in IQ over time in America.

However, a study by Flynn (2009) found that tests carried out on British children in 1980 and again in 2008 show that the IQ score of an average 14-year-old had dropped by more than two points over the period. For the upper half of the ability range the performance was even worse. Average IQ scores declined by six points.

This apparent recent reversal of the Flynn effect in England is confirmed by a parallel study carried out in 2005/6 by Michael Shayer and Denise Ginsburg which gives weight to a key contention set out in this book that educational standards in England are falling as a consequence of the degrading of the education system. The decline in KS2 noted by Shayer, Coe and Ginsberg (2007) showed an even bigger effect than that recorded by Flynn: the 11 year-olds were testing at the level of 9 year-olds in 1976.

The Flynn effect has been widely researched and explored in the context of rising IQs. If environmental factors such as good developmental teaching can account for growth of cognitive ability over time then it follows that poor teaching of the wrong sort can account for a decline. Shayer and Ginsburg found such a decline.

This is a key concept in the argument developed in this book that the English education system could be 'making our kids dimmer' at the same time as stuffing them with qualifications. In forthcoming chapters, I will seek to show that this can be explained by qualitative shifts in the teaching and learning approaches in the English school system arising from its increasing marketisation. The re-emergence of behaviourist, 'drill and practise' teaching has replaced developmental approaches with disastrous consequences.

This is a big claim of enormous significance if found to be true. This book explores that possibility and provides some supporting evidence.

## C 1.4 Council estate life

*In 1958, after being on the council housing list since the end of the war, my parents were offered a two bedroom flat in a new tower block on a huge council estate at Warstock, an outer Birmingham suburb of many square miles consisting entirely of council housing. This council-enabled progression to modern housing was not automatic but required an inspection of my grandmother's Kings Heath house, where we lived, by a council officer to ensure that my mother's domestic standards were sufficiently high to qualify for such a move. Only the 'respectable' working class got the best new council housing.*

*My parents were as delighted with our modern centrally heated luxury flat, with its view to the Lickey Hills, as thousands of others were with their surrounding council houses with neat front and rear gardens. Our estate was uniformly and entirely 'respectable', with virtually all families having a father in work and crime appearing to be non-existent. Like most of my many new friends, I gained access to our flat by means of a key tied to a piece of string hanging inside the door and accessible through the letter box. There was absolutely no suggestion or awareness that we lived in 'social housing'. The flats and surrounding council houses provided large numbers of other children to play with and those passing the 11 plus selection exam were well represented. The number of such children was not far off the high overall Birmingham pass rate of about 25 per cent.*

*A similarly heterogeneous social distribution applied to the adults. Birmingham still being 'the workshop of the world' at that time, the majority of fathers had skilled working class jobs. My father, a toolmaker, was* typical. There were, however, also a significant number of fathers with white-collar jobs and a number of tenants had their own businesses. Most mothers did not work in 1958 but this changed quite rapidly. My mother progressed from a local factory job to working in an office at Birmingham City Council. She was quite typical.

However, by the late 1980s, after a decade of Margaret Thatcher's right-to-buy, the estate was fast transforming into the social housing, high unemployment, drug abusing, high crime and deprivation ghetto now associated with large council estates of that era. This change brought about a decline in the average cognitive ability of the tenant population as the 'respectable' working class was gradually displaced by those in need of 'social housing' as a result of unemployment and growing drug abuse. This decline was accelerated by the policy of selling the best council houses to their tenants. This resulted in the savviest and most aspirational tenants buying their council houses at knock-down prices only to sell for a huge profit a few years later to fund escape to higher status private estates. By this means the most cognitively able parents steadily departed the council estates leaving them to the less cognitively adequate and their children. This process does not require intelligence to be inherited through genes. The result would be the same if cognitive ability depended entirely on environmental factors such as quality of parenting and the physical environment.

Far from being housing of last resort, having a secure life-long tenancy of a well-built council house in a pleasant suburb was a perfectly reasonable lifestyle choice before the massive house price inflation caused by Margaret Thatcher's housing policies, later enthusiastically taken up by New Labour, made it an economic necessity for aspiring families to 'get onto the housing ladder'.

This estate no longer exists. All five tower blocks have been demolished and replaced with a private housing development. Where once the towers dominated the local urban landscape, the new small and cheaply built private houses appear dwarfed by the large modern cars parked outside them.

## 1.5 The contributions of Adey and Shayer

Why do some pupils find some concepts more difficult than others? Does this mean that a child is insufficiently intelligent or is it an issue that can be addressed by approaches to teaching and learning?

Philip Adey, Emeritus Professor of Cognition, Science and Education at King's College London, started out as a chemistry teacher but soon became interested in this general query. It's a question that all teachers must ask themselves. I first became a teacher of physics in 1971 and found myself addressing the very same question throughout my career in schools, which included fourteen years as a secondary headteacher.

Michael Shayer, Emeritus Professor of Applied Psychology at King's College and Philip Adey, produced a series of practical teaching programmes and lessons across a variety of subjects throughout all Key Stages designed to 'make children cleverer, rather than just teach them stuff. The first such programme was called: 'Cognitive Acceleration through Science Education' (CASE). (5.2).

I recommend *Learning Intelligence* subtitled *Cognitive Acceleration across the Curriculum from 5 to 15 years*, edited by Adey & Shayer (2002) for an insight into the profound implications of cognitive plasticity and practical applications of how the learning theories of Piaget and Vygotsky can be transformed into successful teaching strategies and lesson plans.

A *Guardian* article of 24 January 2006 discusses the work of Shayer including its Piagetian underpinnings, and especially the 2005/6 study by Shayer and Ginsburg (published 2009) that found seriously declining levels of cognitive ability in secondary pupils based on Piagetian tests.

They concluded that 11- and 12-year-old children in year 7 are "now on average between two and three years behind where they were 15 years ago" in terms of cognitive and conceptual development.

> "It's a staggering result," admits Shayer. "Before the project started, I rather expected to find that children had improved developmentally. This would have been in line with the Flynn effect on intelligence tests, which shows that children's IQ levels improve at such a steady rate that the norm of 100 has to be recalibrated every 15 years or so.

Shayer claimed that the sample contained over 10,000 children and the results were checked, rechecked and peer reviewed.

Despite the Qualifications and Curriculum Authority insisting that standards hadn't dropped Shayer pointed to A-level maths and science teachers often reporting that their students don't know as much as they used to and to the fact that some parts of the GCSE science syllabus, such as density, have been dropped. "Examiners may well be asking easier questions and marking more generously," he claimed.

Shayer and Ginsburg, however, were careful to avoid any speculation on the cause of this national cognitive decline. Plenty of possible explanations, however, have been proposed from a variety of sources and standpoints. As usual the political left produces social and environmental explanations like poor nutrition and housing. The right resorts to dubious genetic arguments involving differential procreation rates and immigration. It is my contention though that there are wholly educational explanations for what are educational phenomena.

In an email to me of March 2012 Philip Adey wrote the following:

> "you are right about the intelligence problem; the left are frightened by it and the right give it too much credence. I have been trying to argue for years that once you accept that general intelligence is plastic, it ceases to be the bogey-man ushering in racism etc. and becomes a great opportunity."

This 'opportunity' is the central theme of this book together with the disastrous consequences for the education system of failing to recognise its importance.

My central argument, supported by data from real school case studies, is that since the 1988 Education Reform Act our schools have been driven by league tables in the opposite direction to teaching for cognitive development and this is the main reason for the 'Anti-Flynn Effect' of cognitive decline. Whereas it is the least able that stand to gain the most from improvements in cognitive ability it is these pupils that are most likely to be denied such opportunity on account of suffering the most degraded teaching at KS1, KS2 and KS4 as teachers are forced to pursue the Level 4 SATs and the GCSE 'C' grade results needed for the survival of their schools.

My argument is that by compelling schools to be subject to a market in school choice, exercised by parents on the basis of simplistic school performance indicators in the context of privatised examination boards competing to sell their exams, curriculum and teaching methods have become degraded resulting in a significant decline in educational standards. The irony is that the 2010 Conservative-led coalition government under Secretary of State for Education Michael Gove had, unlike his New Labour predecessor, recognised this decline but was ideologically and disastrously blind to its causes.

## C 1.5 Children shun competition in school sport

*This is the title of an article in the Independent of 22 April 2014: "A study of 1,000 eight to sixteen year-olds and a similar number of parents reveals that mothers and fathers are often more anxious about the results of school games than their children are." The report was based on an investigation by the MCC and 'Chance to Shine', the cricketing charity which promotes the* game in state schools. However, almost two out of three children would either be relieved or "not bothered" if the competitive element were taken out of school sport.

This has caused me to reflect on my own experience of out of school sport during my childhood on a huge south Birmingham council estate in the early 1960s. As soon as the clocks went back, and throughout the summer, many weekday evenings were spent playing football on Daisy Farm Park about a mile away. Large numbers of boys from the estate would travel to the park on bicycles, with some of the older ones on small motor bikes and motor scooters. The age range was large and teams could contain any number of players. If there were enough of us we would play on the park practice pitch. This was full size but had a slope and no nets. The rest of the park was filled with flat pitches used every weekend for local league games. If there were fewer of us then a smaller pitch would be created with piles of clothes for goalposts. There were no touchlines.

The main hazard was dog turds, a major blight of my childhood. We hardly ever played cricket and only then in the street with a tennis ball.

Team selection first involved the identification of two 'captains', usually the two best footballers (by easy universal agreement). These then took it in turns to pick the players for their team. If there was an odd boy left at the end he would be allocated as an extra player to the team whose captain had 'second pick' at the start. This ensured well matched teams that would result in a good game. This was much more important than which team won or lost. Both teams would contain boys whose ages ranged from less than 11 to 16/17. Older boys were not overly rough with the younger ones, but it was always competitive in a muscular sense, despite no-one being too bothered about which team won.

The games would often continue until it was too dark to see the ball. At that point the younger boys made their way home but if it was a warm evening some older boys would walk to the 'Prince of Wales' pub across the road, which had a beer garden around the back. The boy judged most likely to pass as 18 (none of us were) would then buy half pints of Mitchells and Butler's mild ale for us at 11d (5p) each. He was always served and we were never challenged. We never had more than one glass each then we all went home. We were never involved in delinquency of any kind (if you excuse the underage drinking).

The council estate girls never played football either on their own or with us boys. When it came to spontaneous games of football we were never bothered about winning or losing, always valuing a 'good game' over which side won. The MCC survey suggests that nothing has changed.

However, when it came to support for professional football clubs it was a different matter entirely. Almost all of us were regular attenders at First Division matches from the age of about 13. I was often accompanied by a *girl who lived in the block of flats opposite. She was as keen a fan as any of us boys. We made our way to matches on Birmingham Corporation buses without adults. Support was split between Birmingham City followed by Aston Villa then West Bromwich Albion. This largely reflected the distance from our south Birmingham estate to the stadiums. The entry price for a child to the Holte end at Villa Park was one shilling (5p). From there, transfer to the Trinity Road stand could be made for sixpence. We were passionately loyal to our teams and great (but temporary) ill feeling could be generated especially after local derby matches.*

*The contrast with school sport was considerable. In the local park we all played football together, grammar and secondary modern boys alike. We all loved playing football regardless of individual skill levels, which varied considerably. At school, the 11 plus selective schools all played Rugby Union and the secondary moderns all played football, so there was strict sporting apartheid. In games lessons at my school at the start of the Autumn Term the Rugby teacher head of PE would supervise the pupils' choice of sports for the Games Afternoons. Except that it was not a free choice. First, the teacher would read out the names of the boys he wanted for the Rugby squad. Then the remainder could choose between various other mildly sporting activities staffed by teachers of other subjects drafted into the timetable slot. No-one much cared what these groups did, except that playing football was strictly forbidden. I played Rugby for my school team and football for the council estate team in the local junior Sunday league, when I could get a game, as I was not one of the best players. I was very clear where my true loyalties lay.*

*Is it significant that when children are in control of their own playing of football they readily recognise their individual personal places in the skills hierarchy without this inhibiting their enjoyment of the activity?*

*It is apparent that for me there was a class-related conflict between school and home based loyalties. Clearly this does not arise when children attend local all-ability comprehensive schools. Was/is this a factor in the relatively poor performance of working class children at grammar schools?*

## 1.6 A further digression into the dangers of common sense

It is 'common sense' that grouping children of similar ability will result in better teaching and learning. Similarly, that boys will learn better without the distraction of girls, and that girls will also benefit from single sex groups because 'common sense' says this will free them from competition for the esteem of boys and allow them to learn without the disruption caused by the more boisterous sex.

Isn't it obvious 'common sense' that children with Special Needs are best catered for in Special Schools, and mainstream children benefit from not having their time wasted by the extra attention needed by their less fortunate peers? And it goes without saying that children that are so dim as to be unable to get an A*-C grade in academic subjects like history, French, English literature and pure sciences are much better off, and will cause less trouble, doing easy 'vocational alternatives' instead.

If school pupils are so badly behaved that they disrupt lessons and ignore their teachers then it is also obvious that more rigid discipline is needed with zero-tolerance punishments for the miscreants and more rewards for the compliant.

According to Michael Gove's Free School model, all that is needed to improve schools is to take power from professionals and give it to parents. This further strengthens the market-based approach and extends it to how subjects should be taught as well as to how pupils should be dressed, grouped and managed. By such means 'common sense' should reign supreme and standards will rise as a result of the universal power of market forces.

The Nobel laureate economist James Meade (1977), who died in 1995 wanted the following epitaph inscribed on his tombstone: "He tried to understand economics all his life but common sense kept getting in the way". As for economics, so for education, and no more so than in England at the time of writing this book. I return to this important matter in Part 5, in discussing the work of the 2002 Economics Laureate, Daniel Kahneman (5.6).

There is no educational issue where there has been more argument than that of mixed ability teaching, which has been extensively researched over the last 40 years. There is no consensus on the effects of mixed ability grouping on the attainment of the most able, but there is evidence suggesting that all pupils benefit when taught alongside more able peers. The Cognitive Acceleration (CA) approaches of Shayer and Adey and others stress the importance of the social context of learning (from Vygotsky), and especially peer-peer interactions. This does not rule out setting by ability but CA and other developmental approaches do not involve pupils sitting in silence in isolated rows trying to absorb or 'learn' information.

The English education system has for some time been in the grip of fear of indiscipline in schools, for which common sense dictates ever more severe punishments and authoritarian control. Early on in my headship school, when we abandoned a rigid disciplinary regime based on punishment and rewards, replacing it with a programme of planned teaching of the skills of inter-personal relationships, on the Bloom affective taxonomy model, behaviour improved and both fixed term and permanent exclusions dropped to zero. This was sustained over many tears.

T H Huxley, 'Darwin's bulldog', that great Victorian defender and advocate of Charles Darwin's theory of Evolution by Natural Selection, believed that science was "merely the application of Common Sense". No scientists believe this today. I like to think that Huxley was just confusing 'common sense' with logic. We now know that science teaches us that the truth is frequently profoundly counter-intuitive.

Lewis Wolpert's excellent 1992 book *The Unnatural Nature of Science*, refers to many examples of the 'common sense' fallacy, some of which I draw attention to, along with my own examples in the following list.

> If a piece of string was to be tightly fitted around the 25,000 mile circumference of a smooth globe the size of the earth and then lengthened by a yard, how far from the surface of the globe would the string then stand out? (Answer: about 6 inches).

> What happens to the pressure in a balloon as you inflate it? (Answer: it gets less).

> If you fire a bullet from a gun horizontally across a flat field and simultaneously drop an identical bullet from the same height, which will hit the ground first? (Answer: they will both hit the ground at the same time).

> If you empty a glass of water into the sea and allowed it to mix with all the oceans in the world then dip it in again to refill it, what are the chances of retrieving some of your original molecules? (Answer: very high - there are more water molecules in a glass of water than there are glasses of water in all the oceans of the world).

> When you burn a piece of magnesium ribbon ending up with a pile of white ash how does the weight of the ash compare with the weight of the original piece of magnesium? (Answer: it is heavier).

> If you toss a coin five times and it falls on heads each time what is the chance that it will fall on tails on the next toss? (Answer: 50:50).

> If you add some ice cubes to a tumbler of water what happens to the water level in the tumbler as the ice melts? (Answer: it stays the same).

Adey and Dillon's *Bad Education* (2012) contains many further examples of common sense fallacies in the world of education.

We will return later to the dangers of intuitive jumping to conclusions and the need for slow, counter-intuitive thinking greatly assisted through the insights of Daniel Kahneman (5.6), who is not an educationalist at all.

## 1.7 Bloom's Taxonomy of Cognitive Demand

Bloom's Taxonomy is a classification of learning objectives within education proposed in 1956 by a committee of educators chaired by Benjamin Bloom. It refers to a hierarchical classification of the different objectives that educators set for students (learning objectives). Bloom's Taxonomy divides educational objectives into three "domains": Cognitive, Affective, and Psychomotor (sometimes loosely described as knowing/head, feeling/heart and doing/hands respectively). Within the domains, learning at the higher levels is dependent on having attained prerequisite knowledge and cognitive ability gained through progression through lower levels.

I have set out two versions of the cognitive domain taxonomy that all teachers used to meet in their training before the Gove reforms of teacher training increasingly moved this out of universities and into the 'most successful' schools. The Bloom principle is that the relative difficulty of cognitive challenges can be understood as readily recognisable steps in a hierarchy of increasing intellectual demand. By understanding and mastering the cognitive strategies needed in order to function at each successively more difficult level school pupils can be taught to adopt qualitatively more effective mental approaches to problem solving and the growth of understanding.

Adey and Shayer build on this idea through the learning theories of Piaget and Vygotsky. I argue that there is much in common with Bloom including the need for the function of teaching to be primarily focused not just on the subject matter but also on bringing about the cognitive development needed to mount the pyramid.

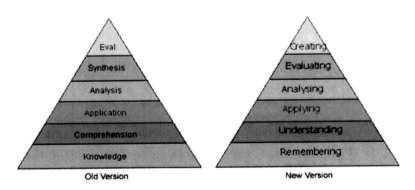

*Figure 1 Bloom's Taxonomy*

The 'Affective' and 'Psychomotor' domains have equivalent validity each generating a similar hierarchy of levels that are also often presented as triangles sitting on their bases. The affective domain has long been neglected in schools, where the development of cognitive ability has to be facilitated in the context of a turbulent ocean of hormones, complex teenage relationships, fears and aspirations.

There are many past and present critics of Bloom, including from sources that generally support my advocacy of developmentalism and condemnation of behaviourism, which are discussed in the next section. Behaviourism often uses the terminology of 'skills' acquired through repetition, punishment and reward. The Bloom pyramid is often referred to as a taxonomy of cognitive 'skills'. One such critic has told me that Bloom was personally a 'behaviourist' (as if this made all of his work toxic to developmentalists). I have no idea whether this is true or not. The Bloom pyramid is, in my view, more usefully regarded as a hierarchy of cognitive sophistication, much more like Piaget's developmental levels.

Critics often confuse Bloom's taxonomy as a 'learning theory' and then accuse it of lacking in evidence. It is not a learning theory at all, just a recognition that the acquisition of cognitive strategies needed to successfully address problems and tasks of increasing challenge is a step by step process.

The most common criticism is to argue that learning is not sequential and that Bloom's Hierarchy seems too artificially constructed and too linear. It is alleged that researchers are beginning to see the mind as more of a web. A person might skip from knowledge to application then analyse the application, come to a conclusion (evaluation) and then re-analyse the conclusion, all working toward a greater synthesis of information.

But knowledge must precede application because you have to be applying *something*. That something is not just knowledge but a *pattern of understanding* based on knowledge. I agree that the upper levels can overlap (or even sometimes be reversed) in ways that depend on the context.

In my view the upper three levels tend to correspond with Piaget's formal cognitive operations and these always build on the lower three levels that tend to correspond with Piaget's concrete cognitive operations. However they are described, teachers are concerned that pupils should progress up the pyramid and most would agree that to progress from the lower three levels to the upper three requires the overcoming of an especially significant cognitive hurdle. I have discussed this at length with a expert teacher of

English as it is from the humanities rather than the sciences that most criticism of Bloom emanates. I was a science teacher. My English teacher friend asked me how Bloom applied to a pupil's ability to extract the maximum meaning from a passage of literature by Thomas Hardy.

My response is that first the passage has to be read (knowledge). Then it has to be accurately comprehended in a mechanical sense - the reader must decode the language correctly (understanding). This understanding must then be deployed (application) to the passage in order to access the three higher levels. The point is that a reader who can discuss literature orally or in writing at the higher Bloom levels has at some time acquired the necessary cognitive sophistication (or learning capacity) through progressing through the lower Bloom levels, not necessarily in an English literature lesson. It is important to note that this progression might have taken place weeks or months before in the context of a history, science or maths lesson.

That is what is so exciting about the acceptance of 'plastic' intelligence and why it is so important for schools and individual teachers to know how to promote it.

## 1.8 Learning Theories

Who needs academic learning theories when we have all been to school and are equipped with 'common sense'?

We would not expect ship design to be solely under the control of managers lacking the profoundly counter-intuitive understanding of the theory of flotation, which emphasises the primacy of the weight of the water rather than the weight of the ship (the Principle of Archimedes). Yet we are increasingly passing control of our schools to managers, on high performance-related bonuses, that know nothing about theories of learning, which are so frequently profoundly counter-intuitive. If such 'Executive Principals' are also running the 'teaching schools' that are intended should take over responsibility for teacher training from university Schools of Education, then sinking standards will be the inevitable outcome.

There is no way I can do justice to the topic of theories of learning in this short section so the following is just a taster. I have arranged theories of learning into just three categories starting with that most commonly assumed by the lay public: the 'common sense' model.

### The bucket theory of learning

In the 1980 science fiction romp *Flash Gordon* (Universal Studios),

Dr Zarkov, a major character, is subjected to 'mind reconditioning' by 'Ming the Merciless' using a 'mind reprogramming' machine. We see the unfortunate Zarkov strapped to a table beneath a huge device that resembles an X-Ray machine pointing at his head. When activated, the machine proceeds to suck out all the knowledge from Zarkov's brain starting with the most recent then going back to early childhood and finally birth. The dastardly Ming then switches the machine into reverse so that it proceeds to refill Zarkov's mind with a new set of knowledge presumably prepared for the purpose by Ming himself. We know this is happening because we are treated VCR style (it was 1980) to a fast frame-by-frame rewind of Zarkov's entire life followed by 'fast forward' reprogramming.

The serious point is that this is an excellent illustration of the 'bucket theory', which assumes that teaching and learning consist of filling the heads of pupils with knowledge. The common term, 'empty headed' referring to a cognitively challenged person, reflects the degree to which this notion of learning is embedded in the popular culture. Pinker's *The Blank Slate* (2002) refers directly to multiple aspects of this misconception. The further assumption implicit in the 'bucket theory' is that, like Zarkov who had to be strapped down, school pupils are naturally unwilling participants in this process and require a degree of compulsion to facilitate the necessary degree of compliance. English literature, especially the writing of Charles Dickens, is full of graphic descriptions from educational history as to how the cruel traditions and theatrical ceremonies of schooling have evolved so as to bring about this compliance.

## Behaviourism

Behaviourism is a school of psychology, very influential from the 1920s to the 1960s, that rejected the study of the mind as unscientific, and sought to explain all the behaviour of organisms, including humans, with laws of stimulus-response conditioning. The principal proponent is B.F. Skinner, who explains his position in *The Behaviour of Organisms* (1991).

Whereas no modern educators would admit to believing in the bucket theory, this is not the case with behaviourism. In terms of the recent history of the English education system, it can be largely documented through the return of behaviourism to mainstream practice in our secondary schools, as well as its resurgence in the primary phase, where many would argue it has always had a partially justifiable role in terms of teaching infant and junior children positive habits and social conventions. The recent further march of behaviourism in the school system is a major theme of this book and one of my principle explanations for the documented decline in our national education standards.

In *The Blank Slate* (2002), Steven Pinker writes: "Strict behaviourism is pretty much dead in psychology, but many of its attitudes live on."

Indeed they do. With regard to the English education system they are being resurrected at a worrying rate.

In Chapter 10 of *Learning Intelligence* (Adey, P. Shayer, M., 2002), Michael Shayer writes as follows:

> Children, like pigeons and rats, can be taught (according to behaviourism) any behaviour one chooses provided it is broken down into small enough steps, each of which can be drilled until automatic.
>
> The implicit model of the brain is a tabula rasa (blank slate), upon which the teacher is exhorted to write by putting the desired knowledge in front of the children.

Behaviourism also provides the methods needed to subdue and control the recipients so that the necessary absorption can be implemented. This is its sinister side.

Behaviourism is therefore similar to 'The Bucket Theory', but with the addition of sophisticated reinforcement techniques using the stimulus-response strategies learned from experiments on animals in cages. Behaviourism is not confined to the world of education. It also provides the theoretical justification for the mainstream private sector management and employment practices based on 'performance related pay', that are now increasingly being applied to teachers in English state schools through the vanguard examples of 'business model-led' Academies. We can expect many of the new 'Free Schools' to be set up on the same basis.

This is another major theme of this book.

## 1.9 Developmental Theories of Learning

Here I include not just Piaget and Vygotsky but all the many theorists that share the position that the mind is more than a collection of memories that include pain and pleasure, but is a self-learning manifestation of the brain, a physical organ that grows in analytical and predictive power through both genetically programmed natural biological development and crucially also through interaction with the material world through the senses. These too are hard wired in the brain by evolution to produce spontaneous subconscious abilities to selectively make sense of input data. The recommendations of the Bloom committee (1956) and those of Shayer & Adey, together with the vast majority of other significant contemporary learning theory contributors, start from this now mainstream common understanding of the basis of learning.

The following quotation from Vygotsky (1986) that summarises the limitations of behaviourism in explaining higher level cognitive processes, is key.

> As we know from investigations of concept formation, a concept is more than the sum of certain associative bonds formed by memory, more than a mere mental habit; it is a genuine and complex act of thought that cannot be taught by drilling, but can only be accomplished when the child's mental development has itself reached the requisite level.

This statement summarises and supports the major theme of this book; that developing the intellect of school pupils in order to facilitate ever more complex concept formation should be the prime object of the school curriculum in all phases and for children of all abilities.

## 1.10 The history of GCSE grades

The function of the exam system is surely to help children learn. This was certainly evident in the variety of assessment vehicles that were used in the early years of GCSEs. What has happened as the government has become increasingly involved? Has the high stakes role of GCSEs as a performance indicator of schools and teachers compromised their function in supporting high quality learning?

The astonishing grade inflation that has been a feature of the English education system since 1988 demands both recognition and an explanation.

It is informative to consider the proportion of the normal cognitive ability distribution (percentile) that historically each grade was meant to reflect.

The GCSE, introduced in 1988, is the direct descendant of GCE. GCE was for grammar school pupils selected by ability. Before comprehensive re-organisation, the 11+ exam (a crude cognitive ability test) usually sought to select around the top 20% of the cognitive ability range in each Local Authority area. This could vary depending on the proportion of grammar school places available compared to the total pupil population. In general, grammar school pupils were expected to 'pass' at GCE at age 16, with a pass defined as grades A-C. Two lower grades D & E were also provided. The C grade at GCE was therefore aimed at the top 20% of the pupil population (80th percentile). It should be noted that not all grammar school pupils obtained pass grades at GCE so the proportion of the national population gaining a C or better through the grammar school system was less than 20%.

The new comprehensive schools that began to be created in the late 1960s furthered the development of the Certificate of Secondary Education (CSE), first introduced in 1965, which ran in parallel with GCE until the two exams were combined into the 'Common Exam at 16' in 1988, which was called the GCSE. I have been a Chief Examiner in both the CSE and GCSE systems. The CSE grade system was overtly percentile based with Grades 1 – 5 defined by the following 'fixed percentile points'.

Grade 1 Equivalent to GCE grade C (therefore approximating to the 80th percentile)

Grade 4 The grade which a pupil of average ability (50th percentile) could be expected to achieve on completing a competently taught course of study.

Grade 5 The lower limit of Grade 5, and therefore the CSE system, was intended to be at the 40th percentile. This meant that the CSE was aimed only at the top 60 percent of the comprehensive school population. Pupils below this level were deemed to be 'non-exam'.

Grades 2 and 3 were awarded on the basis of dividing the total population achieving between the Grade 1 threshold and the top mark for Grade 4 into two equal size groups. This principle was then applied so as to arrange the other grade boundaries to result in each grade 2-5 having the same numbers of pupils. In percentile terms the CSE exam grades were therefore designed to approximately reflect the percentiles shown in the table.

The GCSE combined the GCE and CSE grading system as follows:

| GCSE | GCE | CSE | Percentile |
|------|-----|-----|------------|
| A | A | | 90? |
| B | B | | 85? |
| C | C | 1 | 80 |
| D | D | 2 | 70 |
| E | E | 3 | 60 |
| F | | 4 | 50 |
| G | | 5 | 40 |

*Figure 2 GCSE and CSE grading system*

As soon as the first GCSE results came out in 1988 teachers realised that the value of the C grade had in fact been devalued. The consensus at that time amongst teachers was that the new C grade at GCSE was about equivalent to a D at GCE (Grade 2 at CSE). No-one worried too much about this at the time. With hindsight this was a modest change in the light of the truly epic scale of grade inflation that was to follow. More unfortunately a wide section of the teaching profession, including the teaching unions, became increasingly trapped into having to deny this, even though it has long been obvious to everybody involved in the education system. The most frequent defence of what was happening was the resort to the 'how hard the pupils had worked' argument, articulated by media coverage of pupils opening their results envelopes every August.

The passing of the 1988 Education Act brought about the next major change in the assumptions of grading. Schools soon had to compete in league tables based on the proportion of pupils in the school achieving 5+A-C passes at GCSE. Following the election of New Labour in 1997, any school that failed to achieve 25 percent 5+A*-C (the first floor target) was deemed to be failing by definition, regardless of the average cognitive ability of its intake.

This sought to deny any direct link between pupil cognitive ability and exam performance and placed responsibility for obtaining C+ GCSE results squarely with the school. Failure to obtain at least a C grade at GCSE was at first blamed on 'low expectations' on the part of teachers, which conveniently fed into the 'SAD' thesis, with schools and teachers accused of fulfilling the role of the educational jailors of pupils locking them into the class defined prisons they were born into.

This vilification of comprehensive schools serving areas of social and economic deprivation and their teachers has persisted ever since with all attempts at a defence being condemned as 'making excuses for failure'. So-called evidence for this alleged failure was regularly churned out in the form of the persistently poor results of pupils from poor communities compared to their more affluent peers (the 'attainment gap'). That there might be significant differences in average cognitive ability between school admission cohorts was never considered, investigated or controlled for.

Later, as a high proportion of schools still failed to meet the floor target despite expectations and exhortations raised to 'Masterchef' levels, and a huge increase in education spending by the Labour government, the blame increasingly became shifted towards 'irresponsible parents' who were condemned for locking their children into their own class-defined underachievement as a result of antisocial and dysfunctional parenting. By now, high % 5+A-C = good school, low % 5+A-C = bad school, became the established assumption that leaked from the education pages of the quality press to the aspirational property pages and TV shows that fuelled two decades of ultimately disastrous house price inflation turning this completely irrational and false assumption about school quality into an accepted fact of everyday discourse. Thus to the disaster of lack of access to housing has been added the catastrophe of schools 'failing by definition'.

The Education sections of the *Guardian* and *Independent* regularly featured schools that had been miraculously 'turned round' by new heads and the government introduced a new annual league table of 'most improved' schools based on annual gains in the % 5+A*-C figure. Topping the annual 'most improved' table almost guaranteed such an article. This annual 'miracle' was first debunked by research commissioned by the *TES* in 2005 (Titcombe & Davies).

With no link recognised between pupil cognitive ability and exam performance and with privatised exam boards competing for 'business' from potentially sub-floor target schools threatened with closure and with all schools now competing in the league table jungle for bright pupils, grade inflation soon became so rampant that a new A* grade became necessary to divide up the increasing proportion of pupils being graded at A.

The C grade then became the grade an average pupil should expect to attain. Before long the 'average' became dropped and the C grade became the 'expected' grade for all secondary pupils (alongside SATs Level 4 for primary pupils). This reduced the C grade threshold at first to the average, 50th percentile (former CSE Grade 4 – below GCE 'E' Grade equivalence), rather than the 80th percentile required for 'matriculation' in the GCE system. Later, when English and maths were made compulsory within the 5+A*-Cs needed for league tables, the C grade was further devalued to become the 'expected' grade for acceptable literacy and numeracy, the assumption being that all pupils should be able to achieve this if attending any school with acceptable standards. This in effect reduced the C grade to well below the 40th percentile (CSE grade 5).

## 1.11 The C grade and Bloom's taxonomy

In the days of GCE, when C grades were required for university 'matriculation' and less than 20 percent of the school population was admitted to the much smaller number of universities that now exist, it is apparent that Level 3 of Bloom (Application) must have been a minimum requirement. Studies of GCE exam papers from the 1960s and 70s show that a high proportion of questions were at or above the tier three 'Application' level in Bloom.

The introduction of General National Vocational Qualifications (GNVQs), which were equivalent to up to 4xC grade GCSEs, in the late 1990s brought an accelerated race to the Bloom basement in classroom practice. These 'vocational' qualifications were awarded with no requirement for the demonstration of any cognitive ability at all. Not even Level 1 Bloom (Remembering) was required as there were no formal examinations and validation merely required the teacher to tick a box indicating that the pupil had been exposed to a particular 'experience' or context. This therefore placed the C grade 'vocational equivalent' at 'Sub-Bloom', where it remained until the 2012 reforms introduced by Michael Gove to take effect from 2014, GNVQ having been already replaced with many hundreds of such GCSE 'equivalent' qualifications from 'Horse Care' to 'Hospitality', taking in 'Nail Care' on the way.

Current GCSE exams make varying levels of cognitive demand, but it has become increasingly possible to obtain a C grade without even attempting any questions above Bloom Level 2 (Understanding) and this is especially the case for English and maths, the essential subjects for driving league tables. Indeed it would appear that Level 1 (Remembering) now predominates in these subjects opening the door to the resurfacing of the long discredited drill and practice teaching methods of behaviourism.

Exams that require only Bloom Level 1 are most cost effectively taught by Skinner-type Behaviourist methods involving practising (drilling), cramming, revision, rewards and punishments, with ever harsher disciplinary and sanctions based school regimes required to contain the resulting disaffection.

To explore what this now means in terms of the minimum cognitive ability required to achieve a C grade in maths and English, we can take the example of Mossbourne Community Academy, a school with an intake that corresponds with the national cognitive ability distribution, which achieved 82% 5+A*-C including English and maths in 2010. This means that 82% of the national average Mossbourne pupils must have obtained a GCSE grade C in maths, making the 18th percentile the C grade threshold. This translates into a cognitive ability score of 87. When the GCSE was created such a pupil would have been deemed to have a cognitive ability below the minimum for Grade G.

This means that government education policies since the 1988 Education Act have either been disastrous or miraculous in their effect. We have either suffered education-destroying grade inflation, or schools have enabled the cognitive ability level at which a C grade in maths becomes accessible to drop from the 80th to well below the 40th percentile.

Bloom's Taxonomy, if used to assess the cognitive demand of current exams, offers one possible tool for determining whether this change in the status of the C grade reflects the disastrous outcome of extreme grade inflation. Has deep learning of the sort demanded by the upper levels of Bloom's Taxonomy been abandoned by schools or have the educational reforms of successive governments triumphantly succeeded? The work of Flynn, Adey, Shayer, Ginsburg, and so many others in our universities point clearly to the former.

An educational catastrophe has been taking place in the English education system driven by the false but popular assumption that competition and choice will raise standards.

*Part 2*

*The Consequences of 'Bad Education'*

## 2.1 Educational Failure – 'by definition'

Since 1997 schools have come to be defined as failing if less than an arbitrary proportion of pupils decreed from time to time by the Secretary of State for Education, achieves at least 5 'good' grade GCSE passes. By 'good' grades is meant A*-C. It follows therefore that grades below C must be 'bad' grades, regardless of the degree of cognitive progress such a grade may represent for the individual pupil. The Blair Labour government initiated this approach with a 'failing school' threshold of 25 percent. It was euphemistically called the 'Schools in Challenging Circumstances Initiative'.

The DfE School Performance Tables now contain interesting extra data. 'Average KS4 exam entries per pupil' is one example. This is given for pupils designated Low, Middle and High attainment on entry in Y7 based on KS2 SATs levels. Low = less than Level 4, Middle = Level 4, High = Level 5 and above.

The following are the average entries per pupil data for a real school that was graded 'Outstanding' by OfSTED.

GCSE entries only                  Entries including 'equivalents'

| <L4 | L4 | L5+ |
|---|---|---|
| 3.2 | 6.0 | 8.6 |

| <L4 | L4 | L5+ |
|---|---|---|
| 15.2 | 17.6 | 19.2 |

*Figure 3 GCSE entries for an outstanding school*

Consider an imaginary pupil, 'Janet', who entered the school with SATs L3, and 'John' who entered this school with SATs L4. John finds himself predicted to get mainly C grades at GCSE, but Janet is predicted to get Ds and Es. All pupils have to take English and maths GCSEs, but whereas John is allowed to take four other GCSE subjects, Janet is not allowed to take any other GCSE subjects at all; not even science. However both pupils take one or more 'vocational equivalent' courses, which each produce up to four 'C' grades that count for league tables. As the second table shows taking these courses can run up large numbers of subject entries. Some of Janet's friends also with L3 SATs are allowed to take some more GCSEs. So why is this 'outstanding' school designating a different curriculum for Janet compared to John in terms of GCSE (not equivalents) courses taken?

The false assumption was and remains that all pupils should be able to achieve a C grade at GCSE, thus denying the bell curve cognitive ability distribution that describes the fact of human variation. The first perverse consequence was the general degrading of the school curriculum through the now almost universally acknowledged scam of the General National Vocational Qualification (GNVQ) 'vocational equivalents'. This rapidly resulted in a tsunami of 'school improvement', first exposed through my work with my statistician colleague (Titcombe & Davies 2006) for the *TES*. Our co-worker at *TES* during 2005 was the educational journalist and author Warwick Mansell, author of the excellent *Education by Numbers -The Tyranny of Testing* (2008), which sets out a detailed and well-argued complementary narrative that could be usefully read alongside this book.

The first attempt to mitigate the vocational scam was the inclusion of English and maths in the headline league table performance indicator. The discredited GNVQ was soon abolished in name, but in reality hugely expanded in the form of a large number of other 'vocational courses' promoted by the examination boards. The result was the degrading of GCSE English and maths through grade inflation (1.10, 5.1) so as to avoid the politically damaging collapse of national school exam results that would otherwise have been the inevitable consequence because C grade pass rates in English and especially maths lagged well behind the new vocational inflated average 5+A*-C figures.

The 2010 Conservative-led coalition government soon moved to end the vocational scam. This was fully justified by the conclusions of the Wolf Report (2011). However, until 2014 it could still be exploited to virtually guarantee every pupil the achievement of GCSE C grade 'equivalents' in the other three subjects needed for the league tables alongside English and maths. This made C grades in English and maths crucial, so further raising the stakes for C grade success in these vital core subjects. The consequences of this are explored in Part 3.

Regardless of 'Janet's' employment prospects, she is fairly likely to become a mother and if she does, she will be much more likely than her male partner to take the main caring role for her children.

One of the statistical patterns with the strongest and most persistent predictive power is that which links the performance of children at school with the educational attainment of their mothers. As Vygotsky (5.2) said, habits of mind are contagious; presumably none more so than in passing learning habits from parent to child.

So far as the parental role is concerned, a broad and balanced education resulting in mainly D grade GCSEs is not so significantly worse than one that results in C grades, and a lot better than a narrower curriculum diet of 'vocational equivalents'. However it is catastrophically worse for the school.

'Outstanding' school judgements from OfSTED and league table respectability need C grades. D grades are useless for these purposes. Not so for the parental role however. The problem of a curriculum dominated by vocational equivalents is not so much their limited knowledge content as with the associated learning process. This could be described as lacking in the potential for developing the capacity for future learning, which I take to mean developing plastic intelligence (1.5, 5.2, 5.5).

The Part 4 Case Study exposes the myth of 'challenging circumstances' (the SAD thesis described in Part 1) as the explanation for relatively poor exam results by showing that it is not primarily social and economic factors but, in terms of what can be measured, general cognitive ability, that is the main driver of pupil and school performance. This counter-intuitive fact, so uncomfortable to the political left, was revealed in America by Herrnstein and Murray in *The Bell Curve* (1992), through the availability of IQ type data that could be cross referenced with various outcomes including socio-economic data and pupil performance in the school system.

The socio-economic profile of the Mossbourne Community Academy intake, explored in Part 4, is poor yet the school obtains outstanding GCSE and A Level results for its pupils. This success is regularly trumpeted by the proponents of the Academies programme, usually without mentioning that it is made possible through intake selection on the basis of Cognitive Ability Test (CAT) scores.

SAD (1.4) predicts that bright pupils with high CAT scores from deprived postcodes should be expected to underperform their CAT score performance. The Mossbourne study shows that in a good comprehensive school they don't.

The SAD assumption fallacy is only revealed through CAT testing. Mossbourne uses CATs to select a national normal CAT score distribution of socially deprived pupils that, well taught, turn out to perform just as well as any other nationally representative CAT score cohort of pupils. The downside is that there is a large excess of low CAT score pupils from the Mossbourne community that can't get into their local school. This is repeated all over the country wherever Academies with banded admission policies driven by CATs, located in socially deprived areas, outperform their local community schools that are not allowed to reject the excess of lower ability applicants. The wider success of the Mossbourne model comes from the fact that CATs testing in Year 6 of primary school is universal in Hackney with the result that all the secondary schools in the system benefit from having intakes with a better ability balance than would be case if only some of the schools had banded admissions policies.

Despite the best efforts of the exam boards and the expensive courses the examiners ran for teachers to tip them off on what the exam questions would be (exposed by the *Daily Telegraph* in 2011), there will always be a proportion of pupils of lower cognitive ability in comprehensive schools that persist in showing little promise of achieving the C grade target by the end of Year 11 no matter how much the C grade is devalued, how hard they try or however rigorously they are coached and crammed. The shape of the intake ability distribution dictates that the lower the mean cognitive ability in the community served by the school, the greater the number of sub-C grade 'no hopers' there will be in a school.

Far from being a sign of failure on the part of anybody such a continuously variable exam performance *should* be the outcome of any sound exam system. The 2010 coalition government, like its Labour predecessor, wrongly persisted in regarding this as an 'achievement gap' related to social disadvantage that has to be closed, rather than an outcome attainment spectrum consequent upon predicable natural variation in cognitive ability. The 'achievement gap' between the bottom and the top of a normal bell curve distribution cannot be 'closed' without lowering overall standards and inflicting damage on the education system. This is a major theme running through this book.

CAT scores accurately predict the exam results of cohorts of pupils (the larger the cohort, the better the prediction) in all exams that validly test general reasoning ability. The greater the cognitive challenge of particular subjects, the better the prediction. As cognitive ability is continuously variable according to the bell curve, so should be pupil performance in exams. There is therefore no obvious threshold of attainment that indicates an 'acceptable', and still less, an 'expected' level of performance at any given age. Part 1 explains from a historical perspective why any average or 'expected' level could not in any event be anywhere near the GCSE 'C' grade without doing great violence to the assumption of the maintenance of standards over time (1.10).

As for GCSE in the secondary phase, so for Key Stage 2 (KS2) tests in primary schools. As there can be no 'expected level' in a continuous distribution, the government 'expectation' of at least Level 4 for all pupils has no validity either.

This statistical truth is usually dismissed and scorned as 'making excuses for failure'. However if the fact of continuously variable general intelligence is recognised the focus of schooling can and should change to raising the cognitive ability of the national pupil population as a whole. In most of this book I describe this process in terms of 'cognitive ability' that can be measured with CATs tests. In 5.5 I refer to a parallel discourse favoured by Guy Claxton that develops the concept of 'learning capacity'. To avoid confusion, it is important to note that for me, 'cognitive ability', 'plastic intelligence', and 'learning capacity' are all closely related and are all promoted by the developmental approaches to teaching and learning that are described in Part 5.

The solution to unacceptably low standards towards the bottom of the bell curve is not to try to 'close the gap', or mathematically impossible attempts 'to bring the poorer achievers up to the average', but to raise educational standards for all pupils of all abilities, while addressing specific gaps in knowledge and understanding.

In other words we must stop trying to deny the bell curve, or attempting to squash the ends into the middle, but lift it as a whole to higher levels for all pupils of all abilities. Slower learners may justify greater investment in aspects of their learning development to help them overcome some specific hurdles that are a feature of modern life, but not for the purpose of reducing the 'gap' between the highest and lowest achievers.

## 2.2 The educational and social consequences of 'failure by definition'

If a school is *defined* as failing for not getting pupils to achieve a C grade in English and maths, what does this say for the pupils that find themselves in this shameful category that is causing the failure of their school and the negative labelling of their communities? The failure label will not be new to most of those involved. The whole of the English education system is now structured with threshold

'Levels' that all children, regardless of cognitive ability, are 'expected' to achieve from the age of three. In Y6, at the close of the primary phase of education the 'expected' attainment in the compulsory SATs exams is Level 4. As with secondary schools and GCSEs five years later, primary schools are designated as failing if they do not achieve the latest arbitrary target for the proportion of pupils 'expected' to achieve L4. A persistent proportion of children, especially in poor areas, fall into this failure category regardless of how obedient they are, however much they strive and how many hours, days and months of drilling and revision they have been subject to, only to find themselves on the same relentless treadmill towards GCSE 'failure' in their new secondary school.

## 2.3 The creation and growth of a cognitive underclass

On 16 January 2011, BBC Newsnight featured unofficial exclusions from Academies and the effect this was having on the proportions of pupils not entered for GCSE English and maths.

The BBC had researched the following data based on the 2010 GCSE results:

> In Academies 3.5 percent of pupils were not entered for English and maths GCSEs compared to 2.0 percent in Local Authority Community Schools.

> 21 percent of Academies had fewer than 95 percent of pupils attempting English and Maths GCSE (more than double the proportion of any other school type). 9 percent of Academies had fewer than 90 percent of pupils attempting English and Maths GCSE (more than triple the proportion of any other school type). 2 percent of Academies had fewer than 80 percent of pupils attempting English and Maths GCSE whereas all other school types had zero percent of schools which fall within this bracket.

When the DfE was asked to comment on these figures the response was as follows:

> We have taken a further look at the statistics and compared the stats for Academies with comparable schools - these are schools that have comparative characteristics (similar levels of deprivation and prior attainment). These stats show very little difference between Academies and other schools.

> 3.0% of children in comparable schools weren't entered for GCSE English and maths compared to 3.52% for Academies. A very similar statistic. And 29 of the 103 Academies had a zero exclusion rate, compared to 31 of 103 comparator schools. Again - very similar. Furthermore the highest number of overall exclusions was in a comparator group school - not an Academy.

The DfE were making the point that the Academy pupils taking GCSEs in 2010 related to the sponsored Academies promoted and introduced mainly (but by no means exclusively) in poor areas, and they seemed to be arguing that this means they have to be compared with similar, mainly Local Authority (LA) schools whose alleged failure was the reason for their introduction. But the whole point of Academies was to do better, not worse, than the schools they replaced. Given that even by massaging the figures in this way Academies still came out worse, it is hard to see the logic of this argument or where it leads. In any event the argument is not about Academies per se, but the system in which they are a part.

Leaving aside that the DfE apparently had no explanation for why much higher proportions of Academies compared to LA schools failed to enter up to 20 percent of their pupils for GCSE English and maths, and the irrelevance of their cherry picking and anecdotal attempt to further cloud the issue, the truly shocking revelation was the apparent lack of concern by the DfE for data that lie outside the indicators used to drive the annual performance tables. The DfE turned a blind eye to the mounting evidence of poor performance in many independent Academy schools financed by the taxpayer.

The key question raised by the Newsnight programme was why any school would not want to enter every pupil for GCSE English and maths. It is not because grades less than C bring down the school's key performance indicator of %5+A\*-C including English and maths, because all pupils on the school roll count whether they are entered for GCSEs or not. Parents can, however, be put under pressure to withdraw a less able, or more troublesome child and seek a place in another school, which *would* improve results.

Unlike Academies, community schools with surplus places cannot resist such parental applications. The only other way to remove poorly performing pupils so as to enhance the school's results is by legal permanent exclusion, but this is a negative performance indicator suggesting poor discipline, and is taken into account by OfSTED in coming to their judgments.

The real reasons for non-entry may be much more troubling and relate to the concept of educational failure.

Unsurprisingly, more spirited persistent pupil failures tend to become alienated and disruptive and they may then degrade the teaching/instruction/cramming/revision environment for all the E/D graders that the school is desperately trying to get up to a C. As permanent exclusion is too risky with OfSTED, a solution is to 'get rid' by arranging various forms of 'alternative' off-site education. The BBC Newsnight programme featured an example of a female student with a Statement of Special Educational Needs placed on a programme in which mainly boys were taught various cognitively undemanding craft skills in an off-site unit run by an ex-army officer. She was not allowed to attend any classes at her Academy school and so she was not entered for GCSE English or maths in year 11. A headteacher on the programme admitted that such practice was common and described it as an example of, 'the dark arts' of headship.

The reason why this is more likely in Academies than in LA controlled schools is simply because Academies, being independent of LA control, can get away with it. It is not hard to predict what may happen in the new Free Schools, which like Academies don't have to employ qualified teachers (or even qualified headteachers).

Given the huge numbers of Armed Services personnel being made redundant and the enthusiasm of the DfE for more military discipline in schools it is not difficult to see where this will lead. The DfE agreed to support just such a Free School in Derby, staffed by ex-service personnel who were not necessarily teachers, but pulled the plug on the scheme in 2014. Behaviourism (1.8) is the essential core philosophy of soldiering because of the need for the instant, unquestioning obeying of orders. There is little scope for Kahneman's 'Slow Thinking' here (5.5). Any trainee soldier that tried it would soon be put right.

As all these new Academies and Free Schools will be adding to the now thousands of taxpayer funded but independent schools outside any local democratic control or accountability, it is very hard to see how they can possibly be effectively centrally regulated by the DfE, however enormous this centralised office of state government eventually becomes. This issue came increasingly to the fore during 2014.

## C 2.3 "It might be best if you looked elsewhere" by Janet Downs

*Extract from a post on LSN in April 2014*

*The Children's Commissioner describes the ways schools can deter pupils they don't want. "It might be best if you looked elsewhere". That's what one school told a parent of a child with special needs (SEN), said the Children's Commissioner. The Children's Commissioner heard evidence of how schools deter SEN children and said parents of SEN pupils had been put off from applying for a school place because of "negative messages".*

*It wasn't just parents of SEN children who could be discouraged but less affluent parents too, the Children's Commissioner found. Many schools required expensive uniform from an exclusive source despite clear guidance from the Department for Education (DfE) to keep uniform costs to a minimum. The Commissioner discovered schools serving the same neighbourhood could nevertheless have very different intakes. This raised the question whether the admission system was contributing to inequality whereby one school had a disproportionate number of previously high-attaining pupils while another had an intake skewed to the bottom of the ability range.*

*Schools had duties under the Equality Act 2010 to ensure they did not discriminate against any child because of background, ethnicity, disability or needs. Admission authorities should regularly assess their admission criteria to ensure they meet their legal obligations, the Commissioner recommended. The law surrounding admissions was ambiguous, the Commissioner said, despite the Schools Admission Code which came into force in 2012. The DfE needed to give clear guidance about what is lawful and unlawful. If it's suspected a school's admission criteria are unlawful, the Office of the Schools Adjudicator (OSA) can only act if it receives a formal complaint. Anyone can complain but it depends on knowing exactly which paragraphs of the Schools Admission Code have been violated.*

## 2.4 Cognitive Ability is Ignored

No mention is ever made of pupil cognitive ability in decisions taken to close allegedly failing schools that do not meet floor (failing school) targets at KS2 or GCSE or else convert them to Academies. Nor does pupil cognitive ability appear anywhere in the DfE justification for the floor targets themselves. In fact the only justification by all the governments from Tony Blair's to the present day is 'zero tolerance of failure'. When it comes to GCSEs this really amounts to zero recognition of the importance, and continuous variability of cognitive ability.

What about OfSTED reports? Again, no mention of cognitive ability - ever; not even in the 2010 Mossbourne Community Academy report where the Cognitive Ability Test (CAT) driven admissions policy is vital to the success of the school.

This omission also applies to the other end of the cognitive ability spectrum. Just as pupils with very low CATs scores are regarded as having 'learning difficulties,' very high scores indicate exceptional ability. Mossbourne Community Academy has been rightly celebrated for the achievements of some of its students in gaining places at Cambridge University but nowhere in the media has this been related to the high CATs scores of its upper band admission cohorts.

When carrying out an on-line search of the *Guardian* in January 2012 'cognitive' and 'ability' came up frequently, however the only reference I could find for 'cognitive ability' in a school context was in an article by the restaurant critic Jay Rayner suggesting that it could be damaged by poor quality school meals, an argument also made very strongly in a series of TV programmes by chef Jamie Oliver who later mounted a strong but unsuccessful protest at Academy and Free schools being exempt from national nutritional standards for school meals and snacks sold on school sites.

## 2.5 The riots of August 2011

A growing proportion of students are leaving school with GCSEs and equivalent qualifications that fail to provide the promised progression to cognitively demanding professions, trades and higher quality jobs. The English riots of August 2011 provided alarming evidence that our education system is producing a hard core of alienated sub-C grade pupils that show all the signs of coalescing into a dangerous cognitive underclass. The prevalence of high youth unemployment and/or very low paid and insecure jobs, despite accelerating economic growth from 2014, has exacerbated the issue.

Over a period of several nights in 2011, unprecedented arson, looting and attacks on the police took place in a number of English cities. Thousands of mainly young people were arrested and convicted over the following weeks, most receiving harsh custodial sentences. The court appearances provided evidence of the educational background of most of those charged. The national media commented freely on the general low level of articulacy displayed and more than a third were revealed to have been permanently excluded from school. Given the evidence presented in the BBC Newsnight programme (2.3) we can only speculate on the further numbers 'got rid of' by their schools without resorting to legal permanent exclusion.

The Newsnight programme suggested that Academies, far from being beacons of free market inspired excellence in the English education system, were in fact the single category of school that was most associated with both legal and illegal exclusions in an increasingly fragmented system.

Using data published by the *Guardian* and school type information from the DfE website, the table (fig 4) was produced showing the geographical distribution of Academy schools having pupils in Y11 in 2011.

The lower table shows urban areas with no riots. Not only do these areas not have Academies, neither do they share the marketisation ideology that drives the English school system.

While this superficial analysis does not prove causality, neither does it offer any support for the notion that Academies in general or marketisation in particular, are in any way protecting communities from the creation and consequences of a cognitive underclass.

In other words I am not saying that Academies have caused riots but it is very clear that they don't prevent them either.

**Urban Areas with significant riots in order of the seriousness of disorder**

| Riot Location | No of Academies |
|---|---|
| Greater London | 40 |
| West Midlands | 17 |
| Bristol | 8 |
| Manchester and Salford | 8 |
| Merseyside | 4 |
| Nottingham | 4 |
| Leeds | 2 |

**Urban Areas with no riots but very high levels of social deprivation**

| Riot Location | No of Academies |
|---|---|
| Belfast | 0 |
| Glasgow | 0 |
| Edinburgh | 0 |
| Dundee | 0 |
| Cardiff | 0 |
| Swansea | 0 |

*Figure 4 Frequency of riots and Academies in different areas.*

## 2.6 Characteristics of the formation of a cognitive underclass

This is what Herrnstein and Murray had to say about a cognitive underclass in *The Bell Curve* (1992). Although they argue from an American context, the relevance to England in 2011 could not be clearer:

> We fear that a new kind of conservatism is becoming the dominant ideology of the affluent — not in the social tradition of an Edmund Burke or in the economic tradition of an Adam Smith but 'conservatism' along Latin American lines, where to be conservative has often meant doing whatever is necessary to

> preserve the mansions on the hills from the menace of the slums
> below. In the case of the United States, the threat comes from an
> underclass that has been with American society for some years
> but has been the subject of unrealistic analysis and ineffectual,
> often counterproductive policy.

The 2010 coalition revealed itself to be very afraid of a growing underclass, whose emergence in the 2011 riots was met with harsh terms of imprisonment for offences that would have been deemed minor or not even prosecutable outside the context of mass rioting.

The left-inclined reader might be surprised that Herrnstein and Murray, who the political left likes to link with the far right in politics, express their fear of conservatism so strongly. This section is towards the end of their book, the rest of which is concerned with how society should best respond. This is where I have my disagreements with Herrnstein and Murray, as I do with our own Peter Saunders (1.3).

Richard Herrnstein held the Edgar Pierce Chair in Psychology at Harvard University until his death in 1994. Charles Murray is the Bradley Fellow at the American Enterprise Institute in Washington DC. They both share a pessimistic view of the plasticity of IQ. I profoundly disagree with them about this. I think it is significant that they have not been schoolteachers and lack any background in theories of learning and how pupils can best be taught so as to understand hard stuff.

They note correctly that:

> inadequate nutrition, physical abuse, emotional neglect, lack of
> intellectual stimulation, a chaotic home environment – all the
> things that worry us when we think about the welfare of children
> – are all very difficult to improve from outside the home.

The English experience of expensive and essentially social programmes like Sure Start has certainly been disappointing in terms of measurable educational outcomes. Dr Christine Merrell of Durham University Curriculum, Evaluation and Management Centre, responsible for a long-term study into the effectiveness of Sure Start was reported in the *Daily Mail* of 19 April 2012 as follows. She said:

> Given the resources put into early years' initiatives, we expected
> to see a rise in literacy and numeracy scores in schools. So it's
> disappointing that there's been no improvement.

The Bell Curve authors were familiar with similar outcomes from the American Head Start programme on which Sure Start is based, so their pessimistic view of the ability of expensive social welfare interventions to raise educational standards is unsurprising. Even if this is true we should not underestimate the social value of positive social outcomes.

However, the interventions developed by Shayer and Adey through the Cognitive Acceleration (CA) movement (5.2) are not social but educational, and have been rigorously tested and evaluated. The lesson from Part 4 (Mossbourne Community Academy) is that rigorous educational intervention of the right kind, that is blind to socio-economic circumstances, works. The key CA claim, developed over 30 years, is that teaching for cognitive gain in any subject context produces improved performance across the curriculum.

So there is hope that our education system can indeed be rescued. This theme is taken up again in detail in Part 5.

### C 2.6 When does discipline at school become abusive?

According to an article in the Guardian of 19 November 2013, "It's around noon at a popular and successful Academy School. Through the glass walls of the classrooms children can be seen with their heads down over their work. Open a door and they will all jump to attention and stand silently, shirts buttoned to the top, ties neatly pulled up under pinstripe blazers. Tight discipline is something of a feature in many of the sponsored Academies of north London.

Strict dress codes, daily uniform checks and long lists of rules about the different types of detention have won praise from some parents, but others believe it has gone too far.

At another nearby academy the behaviour policy says students are not allowed to go to the toilet between lessons or visit a local shop on the way home.

In another London Academy there is a five-stage 'behaviour improvement path' that begins with 20-minute detentions for minor matters such as not filling in a year planner properly, or bringing the wrong equipment, and escalates to exclusion for persistent rule-breaking or more serious offences."

A parent is quoted, "They are all Academies around here or are run on similar lines. There's only one school that isn't, and it's hugely oversubscribed. We're being given no choice about how our children are educated. Why is it only in poor areas that children are being made to do this?"

*Part 3*

*Spectacular School Improvement*

## 3.1 Investigating School Improvement

Common sense tells us that a school that massively increases its A*-C GCSE count in over a short time period must have become a better school as a result of the process. The research described in this section suggests that the opposite may be more likely to be the case. 'Improved' schools may be closing down rather than enhancing the life chances of many, and sometimes even all of their pupils.

Since the election of the Labour government in 1997, there has been a spectacular and unremitting year-on-year increase in the proportion of pupils gaining five or more A*-C grades at GCSE or equivalent extending into the second decade of the twenty-first century (1.10). This paused briefly when C grades in English and maths became required for school performance tables, then continued to surge ahead apparently levelling off or possibly even peaking in 2013 as a result of the stated determination of Michael Gove, the Education Secretary at the time, to inject 'more rigour' into the English education system.

This year-on-year improvement has been incentivised by the annual publication of the 100 most improved schools list comprising those schools with the biggest gains in the proportion of pupils gaining 'five good GCSEs' over the previous four years. The highest performers in the list have regularly achieved spectacular progress in A*-Cs over this comparatively short time period.

This phenomenon was first investigated when I teamed up with a professional statistician, Roger Davies, and with the support of the *TES*, we attempted to analyse the Key Stage 4 (KS4) curriculum and 2005 results of the schools in the 2004 'most improved list'. This work was featured in the *TES* in January 2006 and our full paper *Curriculum Change and School Improvement* was published on the *TES* website. The *TES* journalist at that time, who worked with us on this project was Warwick Mansell, now an independent writer on educational matters.

In our *TES* study we showed that at that time such school improvement was linked to poor comparative performance in

English and maths. C grades in these subjects were not required until later (1.10). We demonstrated this by calculating % 5+A*-C including English and maths divided by %5+A*-C and then relating this to the level of DfES defined school improvement from 2001 to 2004. This demonstrated that the most improved schools were generally characterised by a big difference when C grades in English and maths were included.

We went on to show that such 'school improvement' was largely explained by the introduction of one or more of the newly introduced GNVQ 'vocational equivalent' courses, where a single GNVQ pass could count as four A*-C GCSE passes and where pass rates were often one hundred percent.

We also showed that the degree of improvement as indicated by the place in the '100 most improved schools list' for 2004 was strongly related to the average number of A*-C grades attributable to GNVQs.

Our second finding concerned provision of courses in science, European languages and history. We found a tendency for GNVQ science to replace GCSE science to such an extent that in some of the most improved schools no pupils took GCSE science courses at all. We showed that 'school improvement' was also linked to poor provision and take up of European languages and history and that the 'most improved' schools tended to have the most impoverished curriculum in terms of pupil access to these subjects.

Our *TES* paper is longer freely available on-line, however I used the data and the charts from it in my paper *How Academies Threaten the Comprehensive Curriculum (2008)*. This can be studied and downloaded from the 'Forum' website. The link to Volume 50 where it can be found is here for those reading the e-book.

As well as for the 'most improved' schools, we carried out the same exercise on a control group of 60 schools chosen from the same Local Authority areas but having recorded no gains in %5+A*-Cs in the previous four years. The average performance of these schools is shown by the broken lines on the charts. These show that access of pupils to a full broad and balanced curriculum was increasingly constrained the greater the degree of 'improvement' in the school.

Our third finding concerned the problems we encountered in obtaining curriculum information from schools. We believed the issue of curriculum entitlement to be important and that parents and the wider community should have had access to information about the range of examination courses available in schools, which subjects were compulsory, which were optional, and the restrictions that were placed on subject choice. There should also have been full disclosure of the examination entries and results in each subject. Despite being able to call upon the administrative resources of the *TES* and the Freedom of Information Act (FOI) we had difficulty obtaining this information from many schools. Unwillingness to disclose curriculum information and subject-by-subject exam results was strongly linked to the degree of 'school improvement'. The 'most improved' schools tended to be the most secretive.

I have been researching school improvement, real and apparent, since 2003 and this remains the case. It remains difficult to obtain detailed information about the Key Stage Four curriculum and exam results in many of the 'most improved' schools including those judged to be 'outstanding' by OfSTED.

## C 3.1 Why practical work is vital – and not just in science

On 21 November 2013 OfSTED published a report entitled, Maintaining curiosity: a survey into science education in schools.

They also found that dull teaching – accompanied by a lack of practical work in the subject – was putting pupils off the subjects.

In some schools, not enough time had been set aside in the timetable for pupils to do practical work.

Girls, in particular, were likely to ditch physics – with only 11,390 going on to do it in the sixth-form in 2011 despite 159, 745 getting two good GCSE passes in science.

In addition, a minority of secondary schools were 'pre-occupied with tests and examination results as ends in themselves' rather than aiming to improve pupils' deeper knowledge of the subject.

The report points out that getting good grades in science is not necessarily the same as "getting" science.

All this is true but the principles are general and relate to all learning. Practical work is not just necessary for developing 'practical skills' but for promoting cognitive development that spills over into all subjects and all learning.

OfSTED are right that, 'getting good grades in science is not necessarily the same as "getting" science', but they omit to make the connection that this is true for all subjects. But you have to read between the lines to make the most important inference of all.

When league tables and floor targets drive teaching and learning then there are always far reaching adverse consequences with regard to pupil *curiosity, morale, progression and deep learning. This applies to more than 'a minority of schools'.*

*Increasing diversity and competition in the school system creates just such perverse incentives and it therefore follows that the consequence is likely to be not just poor quality science teaching but a general decline in the cognitive ability of our school leavers.*

## 3.2 Investigating the new Academies

We intended to include the 2005 results of the new Academies in our work for the *TES*, but we were prevented by the refusal of these schools to disclose their subject-by-subject results. *TES* had been assured by the then Department for Education and Skills (DfES), prior to the study, that Academies were covered by FOI. Shortly after the first questionnaires were sent out DfES reversed their ruling and supported Academies in keeping this information secret. DfES then repeatedly refused to provide the information from its own records arguing that it did not hold it. I appealed this to the Office of the Information Commissioner (ICO) but after taking more than a year to reach a decision ICO supported the DfES in its argument that it did not hold the requested information. Even a direct parliamentary question from David Chaytor MP (Bolton North) failed to extract the information (Hansard 21 June 2007). After that setback I tried to obtain the subject results of Academies from other sources with limited success. I managed to obtain the 2006 results for a small number of Academies from Local Authorities and these revealed an alarming pattern of curriculum degradation along the same lines as the 2004 'most improved' schools but with even more draconian outcomes in terms of restricting access to mainstream curriculum, not just to less able pupils, but in some cases to all pupils.

In one Academy, there was no GCSE science at all on the KS4 curriculum: just 1% of pupils gained an A*-C in history, and 6% in geography. This school achieved an impressive 61% 5+A*-C but only 15% when English and maths were included. Despite this in its 2004 OfSTED inspection the Lead HMI Inspector wrote, "Standards in science lessons are rising...". She went on to note that the curriculum was "sound" for most pupils but unsatisfactory for those with Special Educational Needs (SEN), and that it had been "broadened" at KS4 and "unusually" at KS3, "where pupils in Y9 were taking up to two vocational GCSE courses". The overall conclusion was that the academy was, "improving rapidly", the quality of leadership was "sound" and "the new principal is providing good leadership".

This latter is a recurring theme in academies', reflecting a high headship turnover. The Lead Inspector was a member of a small special team of HMIs that was uniquely allowed to lead inspections of Academies. A Protocol agreed between the Department for Children, Families and Schools (DCFS) Academies Division and OfSTED (revised November 2004) states that this select team was necessary, "to ensure that a consistent approach is adopted". Two HMI members of this Academies inspection team represented OfSTED in regular meetings with the Academies Group at DCSF to monitor the progress of Academies and also to plan inspections and brief inspectors of possible predecessor schools in areas where feasibility studies for the introduction of Academies had taken place.

In another Academy, despite achieving 34% 5+A*-Cs, just one pupil achieved an A*-C pass in double award science (the science course recommended for all pupils at the time by DCSF), one in Spanish, and none in history or geography.

In a third academy just 9% of pupils gained an A*-C in double award science, 5% in history, 2% in geography, 1% in French and 3% in German, yet 48% gained 5+A*-Cs. The only comment in the 2006 OfSTED inspection report related to these results is, "The secondary phase curriculum is satisfactory". The judgements on the sixth form were however damning. The curriculum provision was graded as "inadequate, lacking breadth and balance, and offering only a limited range of courses". The Lead Inspector did not make the obvious link between the poverty of provision for mainstream academic subjects at KS4 and the ability of the school to provide a full range of opportunities in the sixth form. The report said nothing about the expertise and qualifications of the teaching staff and their consequent ability to provide a broad and balanced curriculum for all pupils. It was not just the curriculum in the sixth form that was judged inadequate, but also the general provision of education and services for meeting the needs of these learners. This would seem to have been a clear judgement of inadequacy of the sixth form as a whole, inviting the conclusion that the school was failing to give its sixth form students an acceptable standard of education; normally a signal for the imposition of *Special Measures* or at least a *Notice to Improve*. However, this is what the Lead HMI Inspector wrote in her post-inspection letter to pupils:

> We were thrilled to see the huge improvements since our first HMI visit over a year ago.
>
> Your GCSE results were really good.

The principal, the headteacher and the academy leadership team have worked really hard and it's paying off.

Your academy is remarkable.

We hope that your academy, with your help, just keeps getting better and better.

A fourth Academy achieved 50% 5+A*-C but only 18% including English and maths. Compared to the previous examples this school did slightly better in mainstream subjects achieving 15% in double award science, 5% in history, 10% in geography, 3% in French, 1% in Spanish and 2% in German. But compare this with the 2002 results in the last year of existence of the allegedly failing school replaced by the Academy. This former school achieved 39% in double award science, 19% in history, 9% in geography and 10% in French.

A fifth Academy managed to produce only 9% of pupils with an A*-C in double award science, 4% in history, 4% in geography, and just 5% in European languages.

These findings were confirmed by the work of Terry Wrigley at Edinburgh University who analysed 2006 pupil level results obtained from DCSF for all Academies. Wrigley found that of those pupils gaining 5+A*-Cs, barely half had an A*-C in GCSE science, nearly two thirds did not even study a foreign language in years 10 and 11, and only ten percent of such pupils gained an A*-C in French: this is ten percent of those with 5+A*-Cs, not ten percent of the pupils in Y11. Only a quarter of level 2 qualified pupils gained an A*-C in either geography or history, and only half had an A*-C in both English and maths.

No doubt then that radical changes had taken place in the curriculum of Academies, but were these changes for the better? Academies had increased their use of vocational qualifications like GNVQ by a factor of fourteen times compared to the predecessor schools. However, far from radicalising the curriculum, Academies largely concentrated on just two GNVQs: science and ICT both of which were just easier versions of existing well established core curriculum GCSE subjects, but now they were much easier and counted for four subjects each instead of just one or two. When combined with a C in English and maths the league table and floor target drivers were met with just one extra subject needing no more taught time than the GCSE version they replaced. Just how easy was determined by statistical analysis of exam results by Wrigley. This showed that a GNVQ pass was equivalent to about Grade E at GCSE (at that time). Yet each such GNVQ pass counted as four A*-C GCSEs. In 2006, pupils in Academies gained 4712 A*-C equivalents through GNVQs, of which 4024 were in science and ICT.

With only token provision of mainstream academic subjects many Academies must have been finding it hard to recruit or retain expert graduate teachers, increasingly replacing them with teachers without appropriate subject qualifications or even by unqualified teaching assistants. Many OfSTED reports hinted at this. The knock–on effect in the sixth forms of Academies should have been obvious, as were the diminished opportunities for pupils from poorer backgrounds to progress to higher education and especially to our top universities.

It is not just access to a broad and balanced curriculum that was suffering in Academies. When 5+A*-Gs, the level 1 qualification, were analysed, Wrigley showed that a higher proportion of pupils in Academies failed to achieve even this lowest level benchmark in 2006, than in their predecessor schools five years earlier. So despite massive investment by the taxpayer, plenty of time for innovation to take effect and exclusion rates of three times that of state schools, Academies were doing worse with the very pupils (those that survived into Y11) that they were primarily intended to benefit.

Academies are independent schools and despite being paid for by the taxpayer the sponsors have had complete power to dictate how and what pupils learn. Much bizarre and educationally doubtful experimentation was taking place based on the whims and prejudices of sponsors, ranging from the evangelical presentation of religious mythology as historical truth and the discrediting of science, to a belief in the need to rigorously train all pupils in the practices and ethics of free market capitalism so as to properly prepare them for employment. One Academy installed a 'call centre' so that "pupils' aspirations could be raised" by training for this type of work.

## C 3.2 Primary schools: Local authority schools are the most improved by Henry Stewart

*Posted on LSN April 2014*

*Of the 316 primary schools with an increase in their 2013 KS2 results of over 20%, just 3 were sponsored Academies and 13 were converter Academies. Fully 300 of these fast improving schools were non-Academies. (Based on schools with more than 25 pupils taking KS2 SATs.)*

*When primary sponsored Academies are compared to similar maintained schools, the non-Academies schools improved at twice the rate in 2013 – for all groups of schools below 80% on the KS2 benchmark in 2012.*

*Selective use of data by the DfE.*

*These are two facts that are not included in the latest (April 2014) Department for Education press release, a classic in selective use of data. It seeks to show that Academies were the route to primary school success. The press release makes two main claims:*

*1) For the 1,340 "converter" Academies, more students (81% against 76% overall) "achieve the expected level in the 3Rs".*

Note that this comparison is on absolute levels, not growth. The schools encouraged to convert first were the ones rated Good or Outstanding. So the boast from the DfE is the not surprising one that, having converted more of the best performing schools, their results are above average. (90% of these converters are rated Good or Outstanding, compared to 78% overall.)

*2) Of the 570 "sponsored" Academies, the proportion of pupils reaching the expected level increased by 3%, compared to 1% for primary schools overall.*

Note that the comparison is in terms of growth, not absolute levels. The schools that grow fastest are those at the lowest starting points and more of these are sponsored Academies. (In contrast, schools above 80% achieving the 2012 KS2 benchmark saw on average a fall in 2013. 43% of maintained schools fall into this category, but only 4% of sponsored Academies.)

The DfE always does the comparison this way round. It never talks about the growth in results in converter Academies (which are a little below the overall average) or the absolute level in sponsored Academies (which is well below the average).

*When compared to similar schools, non-Academies do better*

The DfE likes to give the impression that the only way to improve schools is to become Academies. However it can only make the data support this view by comparing sponsored Academies to all schools and not to schools starting from similar positions. If primary Academies are compared to similar non-Academies, based on their 2012 results, the advantage disappears.

There were, for instance, 81 sponsored Academies and 1,337 LA schools in the 40-59% range in 2012. The results for the sponsored Academies rose by an impressive 5.3%. However the results for the LA schools rose by more than double that, 12.0%. The same is true of the 20-39% and the 60-79% band. In the highest band, 80%+, both Academies and non-Academies saw their results fall on average by 4%.

## 3.3 The expansion of Vocational Equivalents

Vocational courses on the NVQ model are different in principle from traditional school qualifications like the GCSE. The aim of vocational education is to bring as many trainees as possible, regardless of ability, up to a threshold level of competence. This is achieved by requiring trainees to demonstrate familiarity and competence with a limited number of closely specified scenarios. It is therefore training in how to respond to the circumstances required to be met in a specified job application. This criterion-referenced approach is entirely appropriate to job training where uniform standards are required. Such teaching is structured to make minimum possible cognitive demands and is unconcerned with general intellectual development.

Intellectual development however has in the past always been regarded as what schools are for. Subjects are studied not just for their own sake but also for their value in developing the wider cultural, scientific or artistic understanding of the individual. These fundamental educational assumptions are rooted in the rational values of the European enlightenment, and the comprehensive school movement was about ensuring that the advantages of such an education were made available to all. The levels achieved as a consequence of such schooling obviously depend on the prior cognitive ability of pupils as well as on the quality of teaching so a wide range of performance is to be expected.

This does not mean that broad and balanced education only benefits the most able. A participatory democracy requires the highest possible level of intellectual development in all sections of society. The national curriculum was introduced in order to secure this aim. The difficulties in implementing it with the less able half of the ability range give rise to pedagogical challenges that our comprehensive schools were meeting with ever increasing success before the introduction of arbitrary standards that the government defined as thresholds that all pupils were expected to meet.

By this argument a less able pupil, and society in general would benefit from and should feel able to value, D to G grades obtained at school in mainstream GCSE subjects more than pseudo-vocational qualifications that fail to stimulate or provide intellectual challenge and lack credibility with Further Education providers and employers; despite their having equivalences with GCSE that all sections of the educational community, except the Qualifications and Curriculum Authority (QCA) at that time, came to regard as ludicrous.

This is not to devalue vocational education in general.

Mechanical Engineering is clearly comparable in difficulty and esteem to physics. Flower Arranging, however, was not comparable to GCSE biology, nor was Cake Decoration comparable to GCSE art, and we should have been ashamed of an education system that used such means to artificially boost the illusion of school improvement.

The secrecy that surrounded the KS4 curriculum of Academies, combined with huge discrepancies between %5+A\*-Cs with and without English and maths suggests that at least some of these schools had something to hide. If this was a misplaced suspicion it could readily have been laid to rest by requiring Academies and all other schools to publish their full subject examination results in the annual prospectus, as was required by law until September 2005. At the very least, Academies, like all other schools, should have been required to provide this information on request. The requirement of Academies to comply with Freedom of Information law was only introduced by the new Coalition Government after 2010.

## C 3.4 The pleasure of finding things out

*This is the title of the collection of short works by Richard Feynman (1999), undoubtedly one of the twentieth century's most brilliant theoretical physicists and original thinkers. (He died in 1988). The first chapter of his book is here.*

*https://keepthinkup.files.wordpress.com/2014/07/feynman_-_the_pleasure_of_finding_things_outbookfi-org.pdf*

*Feynman's 1981 BBC interview can still be seen here:*

*http://www.bbc.co.uk/iplayer/episode/p018dvyg/horizon-19811982-9-the-pleasure-of-finding-things-out#group=p01qvnmd*

*Feynman had many talents including a great disregard for pomposity in all its forms. He enjoyed the friendship of people from all walks of life. Should the 'pleasure of finding things out' be confined to the minds of Nobel Prize winners? I am sure it must not. I am equally certain that it is a universal human characteristic to take deep pleasure in gaining understanding and intellectual development from the application of curiosity. Watching my pre-school grandchildren conducting an enthusiastic bug-hunt in the garden convinces me that such curiosity is not only an innate characteristic of the human species, but is also too precious to be dulled or squandered in an education system driven by the testing needed to provide school performance data that drives false 'choice' in a marketised education system.*

*I argue for a broad and balanced curriculum for all pupils up to at least the age of 16. This is because if curiosity is the driver of learning then the full spectrum of possible exploration should be available as a resource to all pupils. I also believe in 'plastic intelligence'. This implies a dynamic interaction between perception and the mind, leading to the enhancement of general cognitive abilities. When a pupil gets absorbed and mentally challenged in (for example) a historical study topic, then she also gets better at maths and science, and vice-versa. This is a powerful argument for maintaining subject breadth in the school curriculum for as long as possible and certainly at least up to the age of 16. Eclecticism as a quality was greatly valued and apparent in the lives of our great Victorians in diverse fields of human endeavour. It is in need of restoration in our schools. The knowledge gained from an eclectic education is important at all ability and attainment levels. Not only do we benefit from well-educated employees and professionals at all levels but even more so from well-educated mothers and fathers.*

*Curiosity can lead along all sorts of diverging pathways. Barrow-in-Furness, near where I live has within the borough boundary an impressive medieval abbey. However Furness Abbey is in ruins, but nearby Great Urswick church, dating from the same period is not. Should every well-educated school leaver understand the reason for that? It is a very spicy story.*

*What is the connection between that observation and the fact that Cilla Black (1960s pop singer who performed with the Beatles in the Liverpool Cavern Club) was not allowed by her father to date boys that attended the 'wrong' school?*

*Labour plans for 'gold standard' vocational courses provided by FE Colleges, for students that do not wish to go to university. This is admirable and long overdue. Just because KS4 'vocational alternatives' were a largely educationally worthless scam for raising school's league table status does not mean that vocational studies should not be satisfying, cognitively enhancing and high status in their own right.*

*Too many former FE Colleges have for too long been pretending to be universities and have lost the plot in terms of what they should be doing. The problem lies in the populist suggestion that school students should be divided into academic/non-academic streams at 14. This is to be a 'Tech Bacc' route to give 'less academically able pupils a meaningful qualification'. This policy aim was repeated by Labour leader Ed Milliband's speech at the 2014 Labour Party Conference. In my view such a policy would be a retreat to the era when 'non-academic' pupils attending secondary modern schools ceased general education at 14, compared to 'academic' pupils in grammar schools who took GCEs at 16.*

*What does 'non-academic' mean? There is no distinct level of performance in any test, that can validly divide a population into academic and non-academic streams at any prescribed level let alone the 50th* percentile as Labour appeared to be suggesting. All you can say is that pupils with lower standardised cognitive ability scores generally find academic studies more difficult. But does this mean they shouldn't be allowed access to them?

Pupils are 'turned off' learning by inappropriate and undifferentiated teaching methods, not by the subjects themselves. What about technology and the arts? Are these subjects academic or vocational? Are we to assume that our most academically able pupils should be directed away from cooking, dance, drama and art, or that less academic pupils don't need to study and understand history, geography, literature, science and a foreign language?

How should a potential 'Jamie Oliver' be directed at 14 years old? The task of the education system should be to raise educational outcomes for all, so producing a better educated and more intelligent population at every level. What is wrong with having well educated plumbers, actors, motor mechanics, shop assistants, footballers, tennis players, care workers etc. as well as more broadly educated teachers, doctors, lawyers and engineers?

Both requirements are achievable within a comprehensive school system provided all schools enjoy genuinely all-ability intakes of children. Is the Tech Bacc to be an alternative to GCSE, A Levels or to a Degree? Is Labour wanting to reform the KS4 school curriculum, Further Education or Higher Education? If Labour wants to promote higher quality vocational education and training post-16 then this I support. However, I oppose all vocationally specific teaching pre-16. There is simply too much 'pleasure of finding things out' standing to be lost without a truly high quality, broad and balanced education for all.

Some argue that abolishing GCSE need not mean streaming at 14. But worryingly a lot of politicians from all the main Parties want to take us back to the grammar school/secondary modern split, but at 14 instead of 11 and within the same school. Conservative Education Secretary Michael Gove really did want to raise academic standards for all, but he hadn't a clue how to do it and he didn't realise that it is impossible within his league table driven, marketisation ideology.

## 3.4 Where Academies led the way, LA schools rushed to follow

Many Local Authority (LA) schools have become increasingly threatened by Floor Targets (2.1). There is now a 'cultural' expectation in the English system of dramatic annual improvement in the league table driving percentage of the number of pupils gaining five 'good GCSEs'. In this Part I deliberately refer to this as 'spectacular' improvement to convey the impression that it is truly extraordinary. Schools serving socio-economically poor catchments that have Y7 intakes with low average cognitive ability were and continue to be especially threatened, so it is unsurprising that the uptake of vocational equivalents dramatically increased in LA schools following the examples set by the Academies.

The essential requirement for league table success in a school with a substantial proportion of 100 percent pass rate vocational equivalents in the curriculum is GCSE maths and English, with maths usually the harder nut to crack. So what's the problem if schools can obtain a disproportionately high number of C grades in English and maths by boosting the performance of less able pupils? Conservative, Coalition and Labour governments have all emphasised the importance of pupils gaining at least a C grade in these subjects treating such attainment as the minimum acceptable level of literacy and numeracy, with the underlying assumption that a D grade is very much a fail in this respect (1.10).

The C grade in maths is meant to imply an overall level of broad understanding of the subject not just the ability to add, subtract, multiply and divide. The emphasis on the special place of the C grade is shown to have little educational validity by the continuous nature of the national distribution of the maths grades. In terms of knowledge and understanding of maths the difference in required proficiency between a C and a D is not necessarily significantly greater or more important than between B and C or D and E. However the C grade has been chosen by successive governments to be the arbitrary driver of school league tables and, as such, is the basis of the government's and OfSTED's judgements of school quality and school improvement.

Without a simple performance indicator it is not possible to have a league table system. Michael Gove, the Coalition Education Secretary recognised this as a problem and wanted the performance indicator for driving league tables to be much broader. He favoured the English Baccalaureate (Ebacc).

However, this still assumed a special status for the C grade against the evidence of continuously variable national attainment in all the Ebacc subjects.

## 3.5 What is the problem with manipulating the grade distribution in maths in favour of C?

GCE/GCSE pass rates in English have been greater than those in maths in the whole post war period of the education system. Schools have generally found it easier to raise C+ pass rates in English than in maths, so new ways of teaching maths to maximise C+ performance have been evolved. The crucial question is whether these methods have resulted in weaker pupils being able to understand harder mathematical concepts, which would be highly commendable, or rather have weaker pupils been trained to obtain C grades by sophisticated approaches related to the structure of the question papers and the grade thresholds.

The following questions and issues arise from the distortion of schools' maths distributions in favour grade C.

In 'improved' schools more Cs usually come at the expense of less Es, Ds and Bs. Are the Es and Ds converted to Cs by applying disproportionate resources on them? Have the pupils gaining Fs and Gs received their fair share of schools' teaching and resources? Is the effort put into raising Ds to Cs at the expense of raising Cs to Bs? Are potential B grade pupils taught the full syllabus, or is selective coverage of the syllabus combined with drilling and revision to ensure a C grade the overriding priority? What priority is it for pupils to be taught so as to understand and enjoy maths, or does the C grade requirement overrule all other considerations? Are exam boards colluding in or encouraging this approach? Has this become a more common feature of KS4 maths teaching?

If even the C grade successes have achieved this benchmark by concentrating on the easier parts of the syllabus, and then by behaviourist drilling rather than teaching for understanding, then this is a mechanism that could explain the decline in maths performance of English pupils in the international PISA tests that have not been specifically designed by competing English exam boards in response to market driven demands to meet the pressing need of English schools to compete in the English league table system. If this reasoning is correct then widespread adoption of the methods needed for league table success and OfSTED survival will be depressing rather than raising standards of maths understanding in our school leavers.

The stakes for schools are very high indeed so no-one can blame heads and governors for opting for a formula that produces success in the system that schools are forced to be part of. Wider issues however relate not just to league table status but to cognitive development, progression to high quality vocational education and training and to access to university for children attending comprehensive schools especially those threatened by the 'failure' label because of their intake cognitive ability profiles and by an OfSTED system driven by the same narrow focus on floor targets.

The social class/parental wealth profile of our top universities and the national interest in terms of our ability to produce a well-educated workforce with sufficient numbers of graduates in the academic subjects needed for economic success and national cultural enrichment all depend on progression to both academic and high quality vocational education. So why are our former FE Colleges so dominated by low level vocational courses of the sort so strongly criticised by both Professor Wolf and Demos? Part of the answer must lie in the nature of their funding agreements with government and the existence of perverse performance related incentives.

It is better educated school leavers across the full ability range that are needed. The KS4 curriculum must enable progression to quality academic *and* vocational pathways post-16. It is hard to see how this objective could ever have been served by drafting the lower achievers into pseudo-vocational courses that had very limited value to the pupil either in employment or general educational terms at the same time as depriving pupils of high quality English and maths teaching in pursuit of maximising C grade passes.

On 22 July 2011 the Secretary of State at last appeared to recognise these issues and ostensibly in response to the Wolf Report announced that from 2014 vocational qualifications would no longer be worth more than a single GCSE. Only two non-GCSEs would count in the headline league table measure; and to be counted at all, vocational qualifications would have to meet a tough set of new criteria. This will have resulted in schools changing their curriculum from easy vocational subjects to prioritising the C grade performance in Ebacc qualifying subjects. If this can be done in English and maths then presumably it can also be done with other subjects as well, but with the same perverse risk of poorer deep learning if the newly acquired high stakes nature of these subjects degrades the ways in which they are taught.

## C 3.5 'Campbell's Law: the unintended consequences of the school testing regime' by Professor Alastair Sharp

*Professor of Linguistics, Hong Kong. Published by 'Slow Education' www.sloweducation.co.uk*

*Most of us have heard of 'Peter's Principle' ("Employees tend to rise to their level of incompetence") and 'Parkinson's Law' ('Work expands so as to fill the time available for its completion'). Both point to unintended consequences.*

*In the educational sphere a new 'law' has been adopted: Campbell's Law. This states that "when test scores become the goal of the teaching process, they lose their value as indicators of educational status and distort the educational process in undesirable ways".*

*Some commentators have indicated that the micro-management of education, and the exam based culture that has developed at an increasing pace over the last decade, has resulted in a distortion of education and a decline in the very nature of the humanist tradition on which many education systems have been based. The humanist tradition in education aims to promote intellectual and emotional development, and aims to inspire an interest and a desire to learn, with the ultimate purpose of teaching the young how to live happier, healthier and more fulfilling lives. There is little evidence that this is what is happening in England's test obsessed education system.*

*Campbell's Law talks of distortions. What kind of 'distortions' have occurred? School league tables, 'payment by results' for teachers and pressure on school students have inevitably resulted in the need to 'teach to the test'. Teaching to the test can be defined as a concentration on skills and activities that increase test scores with little concern for the depth of learning or understanding. This 'commodification of learning' results when education becomes merely a test score. A reduced concern for education is necessary as teachers prepare students for a narrowly focused test on which schools and students are judged. School education and instruction has become increasingly measurement driven – if you can't measure it, exclude it!*

*Test scores and educational standards are not the same thing.*

*There has been a narrowing of the curriculum: music and drama are favourites for neglect. Rote learning replaces higher order learning. Schools have to teach exam strategies and rote learned responses, with more low-level, drill-and-skill teaching. Problem solving and creativity are vital in a curriculum, but are very hard to test. They cannot be tested at all using the most common format for testing: multiple-choice questions.*

*The reports of cheating at a north London primary school in October 2013 were nothing new. 370 schools were reported for cheating last year by the Government's 'Standards and Testing Agency'. The Association of Teachers and Lecturers reported that 35% of teachers felt that testing pressures were so great that they would consider cheating (manipulating test scores, remarking assessments, re-writing coursework).*

*And then there is the problem of marking tests… why are we deluded into thinking that they will always be precise, reliable and valid? Essay-type questions for example can be notoriously difficult to assess objectively. Exams are marked by fallible humans beings.*

*Schools that slip down the league tables are pushed into improving their test preparation. But is this the same as improving the education they offer?*

*Campbell's Law states that: "the more any quantitative social indicator is used for social decision-making, the more subject it will be to corruption pressures and the more apt will it be to distort and corrupt the social processes it is intended to monitor".*

*The clear inference of Campbell's Law is that the over-reliance on quantitative scores as a measure of performance for students, teachers and schools has had clear and damaging effects on all those concerned and the very process itself.*

*And if this were not enough, there is very worrying evidence that exam pressure may be a contributing factor behind the rise in self-harming and suicidal behaviour amongst young people. Child Line reported a 59% increase in the number of self-harm callers in 2010-2011 compared to the previous year. 86% of the respondents admitted that depression was the main reason for calling and admitted to hurting themselves as a way of 'coping'. A survey of 6020 students by the Samaritans found that 70% of those self-harming, with accompanying suicidal thoughts, had stated that this was because of worries about school work and exams. Young Minds, the UK mental health charity, is currently involved in a two-year project looking directly at the damage being done to children by the target-driven curriculum in England. Of course these issues are complicated and suicidal behaviour has multiple causes, not least the strong connections with depression and other mental health problems. But there are worrying connections with exam stress: this needs urgent investigation ( C5.2, 5.9).*

*Is it not time we paused to re-think what is being done in the name of education? Why this obsession with measurement? High stakes exams were never this frequent when I was young. We have always accepted the need for assessment: it can be motivational, as well as judgmental. But over–testing is obstructing education. It is time to do something about it.*

## 3.6 Teaching to the test

The *Independent* of 21 August 2014 carried a claim from the National Association of Headteachers (NAHT) accusing schools of poor quality teaching for GCSE. NAHT further claim that this is a consequence of perverse incentives applied to schools and exam boards:

> "Schools are teaching to the test during GCSE years rather than concentrating on improving their pupils' subject knowledge," a headteachers' leader warned today.

So what is lost by 'teaching to the test'? This is the question that led Philip Adey, Professor of Applied Psychology at King's College, London, to devote his professional life to seeking an answer (1.5). He was a chemistry teacher who became obsessed with the issue of 'difficulty'. Why do some students find some concepts more difficult than others and what can be done about it? It would be hard to find any maths or science teacher that has not pondered this problem, or for that matter teachers of English literature exploring concepts of parody, satire and allegory.

Teaching to the test deflects from the necessity of helping students identify precisely what it is that they don't understand and how such understanding can be achieved. If a student just 'doesn't get it', this barrier cannot be overcome through acts of memory or repetition. Concepts have to be 'developed' in stages, not learned.

But is this a major issue taxing the 'Executive Principals' of our schools or is it a case of, 'Never mind the quality feel the width', the title of a popular sit-com first broadcast in 1967. Philip Adey teamed up with Michael Shayer to develop practical strategies to effectively address the issue of how students can be helped to understand difficult concepts as is explained in their book *Learning Intelligence* (2002).

More recently this challenge has been taken up in the context of maths teaching by Sue Johnston-Wilder (Warwick University) and Clare Lee (Open University). I return to their work in Part 5. This is from their paper, *Developing mathematical resilience* presented at the 2010 BERA annual conference. It can be read and downloaded here:

> The more that we studied stories from people who exhibit mathematics phobia, and read the related literature, the more that it appeared to us that the way that mathematics is often

taught in English mathematics classrooms is an unwitting form of cognitive abuse. Instances of ways of working that seem calculated to cause anxiety are asking learners to perform tasks that require feats of memory at a rapid rate or to memorise formulae without understanding, in classrooms where the mathematics is divorced from the reality that it models so powerfully.

These ways of working have been shown by many researchers (e.g.Boaler 2009, Jain & Dowson, 2009 and Baloglu & Koçak, 2006 ) to cause anxiety. Acting in such a way that many people are made to feel anxious, concerned or fearful seems to us to be acting in an abusive way.

Johnston-Wilder and Lee are protesting about the use of behaviourist methods (1.8) in the teaching of maths. These are the approaches that characterise 'teaching to the test'.

## C 3.6 The realities of school improvement

On 29 January 2014 I posted a thread on the LSN website with the provocative title, 'Is school improvement a good thing?'. In my post I mentioned my research described in (3.1).

This is one of the anonymous responses:

"Roger – many thanks for your post – it contains so much of importance. I completely agree with you about the false concept of 'school improvement'. I can give an example from my own experience. To get the % of maths C+'s up the school employed a range of strategies including the following:

- Pupils began studying the GCSE curriculum in Y7 and as soon as they were able to get a C they sat the exam (many of them in Y8). There were many, many resits until the magic C was achieved.

- From Y9 the C/D borderline pupils were taught in small groups with multiple teachers – all other groups were larger with just one teacher (and the groups got bigger through the year after each round of exams).

- Maths was given more time on the timetable at the expense of everything else. Maths teachers were 'encouraged' to provide daily 'maths intervention' classes in the morning before school and at the end of the day.

- Pupils were rewarded for attendance with free take-away food. C/D borderline pupils were 'paid' with shopping centre vouchers if they got their C in Y10 instead of Y11.

- Pupils were withdrawn from other lessons to do extra maths in the fortnight leading up to the exam.

- Pupils were entered for multiple exam boards.

*- Pupils were entered for multiple routes (linear and modular) at the same time.*

*- Private tutors were bought in by the school to work one-to-one with individual C/D borderline pupils.*

*The overall effect is to increase the % getting C in maths but at the expense of higher and lower achievers in maths. It also impacts on the results in all other subjects because of loss of timetable allocation and withdrawal of students from classes on an ad hoc basis. The pressure on pupils to achieve the pass was immense and destructive and led to lower levels of commitment and motivation in other subjects. Regarding the relationship between use of equivalents and lower attainment in GCSE's – your point about less skilled teaching staff being employed is correct, but a more important point is that once pupils get used to a much lower level of demand in the 'equivalents' lessons they often find it very difficult to raise their game to the level needed to perform in a more demanding subject. 'Cut and paste' assignments and poorly structured, low-level brush-stroke analysis is often sufficient in BTECs but is no good in academic subjects like history, English literature or physics."*

*I am reminded of the oft-quoted aphorism from the consumer finance sections of the broadsheet press: 'If it seems too good to be true then it usually is'.*

## 3.7 Early entry

The 2013 GCSE results generated a debate about early entry. The downgrading of vocational equivalents from 2014 is likely to result in schools changing their curriculum from easy vocational subjects to prioritizing the C grade performance in their chosen Ebacc qualifying subjects.

It appeared that many schools are already anticipating this by bringing KS4 forward to Year 9, requiring pupils to make option subject choices at age 13 instead of 14 and losing the opportunity for cognitive consolidation in Year 9 through a policy of early GCSE entry in Years 9 and 10. Year 11 may mainly be used for mopping up residual essential C grades. Such a strategy would encourage behaviourist 'teaching to the test' in all three years.

It remains to be seen whether such changes will be educationally beneficial or whether they will just represent another chapter in the ever-changing saga of manipulating the curriculum in order to succeed in the league tables and jump the next 'tough' performance target to be imposed upon schools by the Government.

Most of the media discussion following from the 2013 GCSE

results was about Y10 entries especially in English and maths. I also predicted a trend towards the general commencement of KS4 in Y9 with some entries even at the end of that year. This provides for multiple attempts at getting the vital league table driving C grades by the end of Y11 Some schools have been making further multiple entries in the same subject with different exam boards, all at considerable cost to the taxpayer. The result is bound to be reductions in the numbers of students achieving higher grades as subjects are abandoned as soon as the C grade is achieved. This appears to be what is happening.

In September 2013, Michael Gove, the Education Secretary, said that early entries are "damaging ", not in the best interests of pupils and driven by the accountability system, where schools are measured on how many pupils get at least a C grade in English and maths. There are serious implications for progression to A Level studies as pupils with only C grade passes will be refused entry to many academic A Level courses.

And that assumes that after a classroom diet of teaching to the test and cramming, pupils will retain any interest in studying the subjects further.

Typically, students may require seven A*- C grades at GCSE, including English and maths. In addition, a minimum of four B grades may be required and these should be relevant to their AS Level subjects. Some more demanding courses may require As or A*s in relevant GCSEs.

It seems likely that the GCSE subjects requiring A/A* will include maths and sciences with disastrous consequences caused by early entry for eventual university progression in these subjects.

The negative consequences of early entry were recognised by Secretary of State Michael Gove and from 2014 only the results of the first entry was counted in School Performance Tables.

## C 3.7 Pupil behaviour worse than thought

*This was the headline in the Independent of 14 April 2014, following the publication of a report by researchers from the University of East Anglia:*

*"Unruly behaviour in schools is far worse than inspectors and official government reports indicate, according to a major study of classroom disruption out today. Even teachers in the most popular, oversubscribed state schools have to work hard to avoid their classrooms getting out of control, it adds. Hardly any schools are free of disruptive behaviour."*

*Let us try to apply some logic to this paradoxical scenario. Indiscipline is found in the most popular, over-subscribed schools. So how do schools become popular and over-subscribed? Presumably by getting 'Outstanding'*

*OfSTED judgements. Am I stretching this too far by suggesting that at least some schools have been getting 'Outstanding' judgments from OfSTED despite poor pupil behaviour? This seems odd, but I have a hypothesis that may explain this perverse pattern.*

*I am suggesting that this is an outcome of Inspectors making their minds up from performance data, before they even enter the school. We know that this approach affects OfSTED judgements of individual lessons. It is called 'triangulation'. If an inspector sees a poor lesson in a school with outstanding results, then we know that the judgment is 'moderated' on the basis that as so little time is spent in so few lessons the observation evidence can be disregarded. This works the other way too. If Inspectors find superb teaching in a school that fails to meet floor targets, then this must be moderated so as not to get in the way of the 'Inadequate' or 'Requires Improvement' judgment that has already been decided in advance.*

*According to posts on LSN by OfSTED insiders, this happens. I am proposing that the disruptive growth in poor behaviour noted in the University of East Anglia study is real and is a consequence of the increasing popularity of 'zero tolerance' behaviour policies with automatic punishments applied according to arbitrary tariffs. I am further suggesting that such behaviourism in regard to discipline policies goes hand in hand with behaviourist 'filling heads with knowledge' teaching methods (1.8). These are frequently so tedious and boring that pupils naturally become restless and distracted. This generates automatic tariff based punishments. These punishments are sometimes unjust and undeserved because of teacher jumping to conclusions (Daniel Kahneman 5.5) and a lack of proper investigation.*

*Classroom incidents are rarely as simple as they may seem to a hard pressed teacher fearful of losing control, so catastrophic misjudgments are likely. Nothing feeds pupil negativity and infectious sedition like being severely and unfairly punished for something you didn't do, in a system that brooks no argument or debate ('backchat' just escalates the punishment). Lots of 'Outstanding' schools now have zero-tolerance behaviour policies (2.6).*

*These are recommended by the Chief Inspector and the Secretary of State for Education and are beloved of parents. So if a school has 'Outstanding' performance data and adopts the officially prescribed zero-tolerance behaviour policies, then what is a Lead Inspector to do, except fail to notice the poor behaviour or make some sort of excuse for it? This goes with failing to notice gaming the exam system through early GCSE entry and exploitation of easy vocational equivalents to obtain league table advantage.*

*But schools must prevent disruptive behaviour from preventing teaching and learning. Of course, but like so much in the real, complex world of education, the ways of achieving good relationships in classrooms between pupils and between pupils and teachers are often counter intuitive.*

## 3.8 Is school improvement a good thing?

The last Labour government never passed by an opportunity to quote from the 2006 PriceWaterhouse Cooper Report on Academies, which it claimed showed that 'Academies were improving twice as fast as LA schools'. This phrase was so frequently repeated by every government spokesperson that it came to be accepted by a supine, uncritical media as conclusive proof that the Academies Programme was a great success. It appears that this conclusion was based on the headline GCSE performance data that showed a large year-on-year improvement rate in the headline five 'good GCSEs' of the then new Academies.

The role of vocational equivalents and other factors was not considered. I am ending this section where it began; with a reference to the annual publication of the most improved schools. The table (fig 5) was compiled by cross referencing the Ebacc data for individual schools from information released by DfE on 31 March 2011 with the 2010 DfE Press Release naming the most improved schools in rank order. Improvement is defined as the difference between the 2007 percent 5+A*-C including English and maths and the corresponding 2010 figure.

*Average 2010 science, humanities, languages and English Baccalaureate GCSE A\*-C results in the 2007-2010 most improved schools.*

| Percentage point improvement 2007-2010 | 2 x science 2010 | Humanities 2010 | Language 2010 | Ebacc 2010 |
|---|---|---|---|---|
| 30% + (23 schools) | 37.4% | 22.2%* | 20.4% | 5.6% |
| 20-29% (118 schools) | 39.7% | 25.8%* | 18.8% | 7.9% |
| 10-19% (233 schools) | 46.0% | 29.5%* | 28.1% | 13.9% |
| National Average 2010 | 45.7% | 34.1% | 30.9% | 15.6% |

*Figure 5 GCSE Improvement Chart*

Unfortunately the 31 March 2011 DfE information on the national

Ebacc results was incomplete in that data for schools where the number of pupils gaining the qualification is less than three have been suppressed (no figure given). Since these are the poorest results the effect is to inflate the averages. Fortunately, except for the data marked * the unsuppressed true figures are available in the School Performance tables and have been used for this table.

This means that the figures marked * contain a small error and are *higher* than the true figure. However the pattern is clear. School Improvement is inversely linked to Ebacc performance. Therefore in Michael Gove's terms, it was the 'most improved' schools that were most in need of real improvement.

The evidence is compelling. If Ebacc measures the extent to which schools can enable academic progression post-16, and this is seen as good education, then the pressure for school improvement defined in league table terms has been making schools worse and further disadvantaging their pupils.

*Part 4*

*Case Study of the role of admissions systems in successful schools*

## 4.1 Which are the successful schools?

The *Guardian* of 2 March 2010 quoted Michael Gove, the then shadow Conservative education secretary as follows:

> The people I admire most are those doing outstanding things for the poorest children, such as Michael Wilshaw at Mossbourne academy, Dan Moynihan and all those at the Harris **Academies**, and those at chains such as Ark and the Haberdashers, who are driving up standards in the poorest areas.

Michael Gove, the Secretary of State for Education in the Conservative-led coalition government was quite clear in his views about the success of Mossbourne Community Academy and the Tony Blair led Academies programme in general, of which Mossbourne was one of the first.

Mossbourne has been widely promoted in the broadsheet press including the left leaning *Guardian* as providing the solution to obtaining high academic standards from the children of severely disadvantaged communities, where Local Authority schools have allegedly so conspicuously and consistently failed in the past throughout England's urban areas and especially in the London Borough of Hackney.

In January 2011, the Guardian reported that, "Ten sixth-formers at a city academy in one of the poorest parts of Britain have been offered places at Cambridge University".

The pupils attended Mossbourne Academy in Hackney, east London, which replaced a school described by the Tories in the 1990s as the "worst school in Britain". Hackney Downs was closed in 1995 and a new school, Mossbourne Academy opened on the same site in 2004. Mossbourne Academy has been consistently praised by both Labour and Conservative governments.

Some headteachers have claimed that Mossbourne, which still recruits from some of the same areas as Hackney Downs, creams off the most talented pupils, a charge denied by Sir Michael Wilshaw (the Executive Principal before he became Head of OfSTED in

2012). He said 41% of pupils came from low-income homes, entitling them to free school meals, and 38% did not speak English as their first language.

The pupils' success prompted John Bald, a former head inspector at Ofsted, to describe it as "a spectacular breakthrough". He called Mossbourne "the best comprehensive in the country".

On 18 August 2011, shortly after the London riots, in an article co-written by Jeevan Vasagar, the *Guardian*'s education editor, it was stated that:

> **Days after the riots, the picture is very different at Mossbourne academy in Hackney.**
>
> More than one in 10 A-level entries were awarded an A* at a school in a deprived part of the country severely hit by the riots last week.
>
> Every teenager studying A-levels in their final year at Mossbourne academy in Hackney, north London, secured a university place – the majority at the most competitive institutions. Seven have confirmed places at Cambridge and three have places at medical schools.
>
> The school is less than one mile from Hackney's Pembury estate, which was the scene of the largest confrontation during the riots in London last week.
>
> The school's success does not depend on a selective intake. Around 40% of Mossbourne's pupils are on free school meals, 30% are on the special needs register, 80% are from ethnic minorities, and 40% are from homes where English is not the first language.

The picture painted could not be clearer. Mossbourne was not only an outstanding school with excellent academic results, but this has been achieved in the same area, where Hackney Downs School so conspicuously failed. The clear impression given is that Mossbourne has succeeded in spectacular fashion with similar children to those that attended Hackney Downs.

The purpose of my study was to explore the extent to which this is true and to probe the reasons for Mossbourne's success and the scope for replicating it elsewhere.

## 4.2 How does Mossbourne differ from Hackney Downs School?

Hackney Downs school was a Local Authority controlled comprehensive when it closed in 1995. It had a typical Local Authority (LA) controlled Admissions Policy based mainly on proximity. It was located, as Mossbourne is now, close to the centre of an extremely deprived, ethnically very diverse community, where a large proportion of pupils qualify for Free School Meals (FSM) and where many have Special Educational Needs.

Mossbourne is a medium/large, purpose built 11-18 school with an intake of about 200 Y7 pupils per year. It was built on the same site as its demolished predecessor. As an Academy however it has the power to decide its own Admissions Policy, subject to the approval of the Secretary of State. Like many of the original Academies located at the heart of poor areas, and almost all of the successful such schools, Mossbourne's admissions are based on banding, driven by an IQ type Cognitive Ability Test (CAT).

The principle of 'fair banding' is to provide a school with a pupil intake that reflects, so far as possible, the national or local ability variation profile. If a particular Local Authority area produces pupil CAT scores with a mean of less than 100 (the national average) it might then be expected that the mean intake score for each school would match the mean for the LA. This would result in, so far as possible, all schools in an LA area having intakes of comparable ability albeit with means below the national mean. It is only 'so far as possible' because any school operating 'fair banding' has to attract sufficient applicants to fill all its bands. Even if a school cannot attract enough first preference pupils to fill its top ability band, fair banding can potentially limit the numbers of pupils in lower ability bands it is compelled to accept.

This can protect schools located in poor areas from being so swamped by admissions of many lower ability pupils that no spaces are available for more able pupils, resulting in a skewed intake in ability terms that would make it more difficult for the school to meet the government's 'floor targets' and/or do well in local league tables, resulting in a downward spiral towards failure. The first tranche of Labour's sponsored Academies mostly replaced such schools. Many of the new Academies chose to protect themselves from the same fate as their predecessors by choosing to have a banded admissions policy.

This opportunity was not, of course, available to the neighbouring LA schools, which were therefore placed at an even greater disadvantage than before the new Academy competitors were visited onto them. Urban LA Community Schools are unlikely to succeed in competition with banded Academies unless the LA operates a uniform system of banding for all the schools in its area.

In my paper *Cognitive Ability and School Improvement (2006)* I argue as follows:

Systematic standardised cognitive ability testing at age 11 could facilitate a range of improvements to the secondary school admissions and funding systems as well as providing valid ways of comparing secondary school performance. It is cheap and takes up very little of the time available for teaching.

The best approach would be to introduce banded admissions for all schools. This creates a maximum admission number for each ability band so moving all schools in the direction of having pupil intakes that better reflect the national distribution of IQ. This would also bring about desirable social class and ethnic mixing. It would thus begin to restore the comprehensive system. The CAT test could be universally used in Y6 of the primary school. Objections to such testing on the grounds that it would reintroduce the 11-plus system are misguided. The banding process promotes access to all schools for pupils of all abilities. This is the exact reverse of 11-plus selection for grammar schools.

This paper is relevant to many of the arguments made in this book. It can be read and downloaded from this link:

*www.nfer.ac.uk/nfer/PRE_PDF_Files/06_36_06.pdf*

On first inspection it might appear that this approach is being followed in Hackney where, in 2012, all but three of the secondary schools co-operated within a uniform system of banding administered and co-ordinated by The Learning Trust on behalf of the Hackney Borough LA, which was condemned by OfSTED in 2002 as a failing Local Authority. This led to the enforced outsourcing of the education function of the Hackney Borough Council to The Learning Trust, a private not-for-profit company. The Borough of Hackney was the first LA in the country to operate what appears to be a uniform system of banded admissions for most of its secondary schools including all the new Academies, which have opted into the arrangements.

Banding requires the use of a standardised Cognitive Ability Test (CAT). In Hackney these are currently provided by GL Assessment and are taken in October of Y6 in all Hackney primary phase schools. It is important to recognise that banding is driven solely by a bank of three IQ type tests. These provide scores on the standardised IQ scale where the mean is 100 and the Standard Deviation is 15. The three components of the CAT test are *Verbal, Quantitative and Non-Verbal*. It is the combined score of the three components that is usually used for banding. This is called the *triple Standardised Age Score (SAS)*. It is now generally recognised that at the age of 10/11 the results of the CAT test are the best available predictors of later academic performance at GCSE and post-16.

It is important to recognise that banding through the use of such tests takes no account whatever of social factors like Free School

Meals (FSM), ethnicity, language used in the home, relative poverty, parental unemployment or any of the other factors that are widely, but erroneously assumed to be major independent drivers and limiters of school attainment.

## 4.3 The 2011 entry Mossbourne Academy banding system

The defining document for the 2011 entry was the Admissions Policy as agreed by the Secretary of State and published in the Academy Prospectus.

The principle feature is the system of banded admissions based on the results of Cognitive Ability Tests (CATs) taken in Y6 in all Hackney primary schools. This is described in the Admissions Policy as follows:

> All children applying for a place at the Academy will sit the GL Assessments Verbal and Non-Verbal reasoning test for the purpose of placing them into one of four ability bands. Each band will contain 25% of the children applying to the school. Children with statements of special educational need and children in public care (see below) who do not take the test will be allocated to the appropriate band on the basis of an alternative appropriate assessment.

> The Academy will offer 60% of the places in each band to the pupils who live inside the inner zone, defined as living at an address located within 1000 metres of the front gate of the school measured in a straight line. 40% of the places in each band will be allocated to pupils living outside of this. Pupils with statements of special educational need for whom the Academy is named on the statement are admitted ahead of other applicants but will be included in the band allocation for the zone in which they live.

A revised Admissions Policy for admissions from 2013/14 onwards has since been agreed by the Secretary of State. However this study was based on the 2011 Admissions Policy, which was in force from the opening of the Academy in 2004.

The Learning Trust (LT) provided information about Mossbourne and the wider Hackney admissions process in reply to my Freedom of Information (FOI) enquiries. The Learning Trust private company ceased to exist in 2012 and was replaced by 'The Hackney Learning Trust (HLT), in a process that seems to have been a fairly smooth transition retaining most of the staff. HLT is now fully part of Hackney Council.

The first response from the LT Information Officer, was to point out that, unlike the Hackney Local Authority, The Learning Trust was not bound by FOI as it was not 'a public authority' but a 'private company limited by guarantee' under a contract directed by the Secretary of State dated 31 July 2002. However, the Information Officer went on to state that the policy of The Learning Trust was, so far as its constitution allows, to comply with the provisions of the Act. He did state that some of the information that I asked for was not available as they did not hold the appropriate records. I was happy to accept this as the other information provided met my requirements. A number of clarifications were requested and these were dealt with by the Head of Admissions and Pupil Benefits. These clarifications and further requests took up a great deal of the time of this person and went beyond the requirements of FOI. I am extremely grateful for her patience, courtesy and for the information provided.

The third source of information about Mossbourne admissions was the Academy itself. I made a number of complex and detailed FOI requests that were dealt with by The Human Resources (HR) manager. These requests also always resulted in prompt, courteous and helpful responses that again went beyond the requirements of FOI. Some of my requests for clarification arose from my own errors and misunderstandings yet the HR manager responded to these with the same patience and diligence, for which I am also grateful.

I was not alone in finding it difficult to fully understand the complex Mossbourne admissions process as I discovered from my FOI enquiries to the Mossbourne neighbourhood primary phase schools, which form an important part of this study. One primary head told me that he had many requests from parents seeking an explanation of the Mossbourne admissions system and had great difficulty providing one. No doubt this complexity was one of the reasons for the need for a new policy from the 2013 admissions.

According to The Learning Trust, for the 2011 intake there were initially 1394 applications for 200 places (the Planned Admission Number). Each application band should therefore have contained up to 349 pupils (25 percent of the total). It should be noted that naming Mossbourne in any order of preference on the Learning Trust parental preference form counts as an application. The parental preference form provides the opportunity to list up to six schools.

The next step was for the Learning Trust to rank all the applicants in order of their CAT scores and then send this list to Mossbourne. I was provided with a copy of this file (and the files for all the other Hackney schools) together with the final admissions files (all with the pupil names removed). The Mossbourne

Admissions Policy states that only the Verbal, and Non-Verbal elements of the CATs test are used for this. This does not appear to be the case as it seems clear that the combined (triple SAS) score of all three elements (including Quantitative) was in fact used. This was later confirmed by the HLT.

The next stage was for Mossbourne to count down the CAT rank order to include the first 349 pupils and designate these as Band A applicants, and so on down the rank order until all four bands were filled.

This means that it was the relative numbers of applicants with each CAT score that ultimately determined the CAT score boundaries for each band.

However the principle of 'fair' banding is to ensure that each ability band is designated by CAT score boundaries that produce equal quartiles (or for some Hackney schools that have five bands, quintiles) in terms of the national normal distribution or the local LA distribution if this is different. The national normal distribution produces quartile CAT score band boundaries as follows.

Band A: 110 and above

Band B: 100-109

Band C: 90-99

Band D below 90

There was no guarantee that the Mossbourne system based on dividing the *applications* into four equal initial bands would produce these or any other band boundaries. What is clear however is that Mossbourne's band boundaries depended on Mossbourne's relative popularity compared to the other schools in the system and especially the actual distribution of CAT scores within the applications. If Mossbourne could have achieved more applications with higher CAT scores then Mossbourne could have achieved a higher mean intake ability than other schools.

As the Admission Number is 200, according to the Admissions Policy, the final four admission bands should, according to the Admissions Policy, have each contained 50 pupils split 60:40 between the inner zone (pupils living within 1000m of Mossbourne Academy) and the outer zone (pupils living anywhere else including outside Hackney). This means that there were in fact eight admission categories to be filled providing 120 inner zone places and 80 outer zone places as follows.

Band A inner (30 pupils), Band A outer (20 pupils)

Band B inner (30 pupils), Band B outer (20 pupils)

Band C inner (30 pupils), Band C outer (20 pupils)

Band D inner (30 pupils), Band D outer (20 pupils)

To get the 349 pupils down to 50 in each band the oversubscription criteria in the Admissions Policy were applied by Mossbourne. This produced a new rank order which was then returned to the Learning Trust, which collated the rank orders from all the schools. Any given child can potentially get a place in more than one school, but these multiple offers are accepted or declined through a process of iterations internally and then via the Pan-London Register so the child will only get a place at the school offered that is ranked the highest in the parental preference. The Learning Trust then writes to each parent offering a place at that school.

The final stage was to add in the successful appeals. According to The Learning Trust School Admissions Brochure (from the LT website), there were 120 Mossbourne appeals of which 20 were successful. According to Mossbourne there were 122 appeals of which 22 were successful, resulting in a total of 130 inner zone pupils admitted and 92 from the outer zone, 15 of which were from outside the Borough of Hackney.

Although the Hackney and Mossbourne admission system is based on banding it is still not 'fair' banding. Fair banding would require the mean intake CATs score of each school to be the same and equal to the mean Hackney primary schools CAT score. This was clearly not the case because of the continuing role of the market in a banding system based on applications rather than admissions.

## 4.4 Mossbourne's Admissions Policy from 2013

When I started this study in 2011, I could not understand why Mossbourne's Admissions Policy ruled that the band boundaries would be based on *applications*. It would be far simpler and more logical to decide the band boundaries in advance.

This is the basis of the new Admissions Policy, which designates the band boundaries on the basis of the national normal distribution giving Band A, 110+, Band B, 100-109, Band C, 90-99, Band D below 90. This is likely to produce a mean intake CAT of 100, which turns out to be the same as the 2011 intake cohort arrived at by a different process. However, the mean Hackney CAT score is less than 100, so this new Admissions Policy permanently establishes a better than Hackney average intake distribution for Mossbourne.

Other changes in the new admissions policy also potentially raise the mean intake CAT score:

> Priority for teachers' children even if they live nowhere near the Academy. If teachers' children have higher-than-average ability,

then this would raise the average ability of the intake.

Change in inner/outer balance from 60-40 to 50-50. The inner zone has a lower mean CAT score than the outer zone. This is also likely to raise the average intake ability.

A Lottery within zones & bands, so the closest will no longer be assured a place. One effect will be Mossbourne will no longer take so many pupils from the Pembury estate.

I was not aware of the full implications of this decision for the Admissions Policies of the other Hackney banded schools, or how they or The Learning Trust responded to these changes. They are however clearly advantageous to Mossbourne. As all Academies set their own Admission Arrangements neither the LT then, nor the HLT now, can do anything about this.

## 4.5 How would fair banding be different?

The requirements for a common LA wide system of fair banding are as follows:

1. All the schools would have the same number of bands and the same band boundaries.

2. The band boundaries would be designed to provide equal size bands within each school based on the LA, rather than the national mean CAT scores.

3. Each school's Admissions Criteria would be applied by the LA as part of the LA administration of the admissions system.

4. A common system for dealing with spare places and unfilled bands would apply.

A simple approach would be for a school like Mossbourne with four bands and an Admission Number of 200 to operate band admission limits of 50 with excess applications in each band addressed through the oversubscription criteria in the admissions policy.

The current legal status of Academies precludes the imposition of such arrangements by LAs. However, despite being less than ideal, the Hackney system is still a major step forward, in that it is better for pupils and schools than what happens in other LA areas, which is either banded Academies competing with unbanded LA and other schools (LA schools always disadvantaged) or unbanded LA schools competing with each other (advantages/disadvantages determined by catchment area demographics).

None of the preceding arguments should be taken as a criticism of Mossbourne. The Hackney system probably approaches the fairest possible within the current national regulations and the league table driven market system. It provides all schools with a reasonably balanced intake and prevents schools becoming sinks in which fully comprehensive provision is impossible.

## 4.6 Information provided by the Mossbourne local primaries

Hackney is a compact and densely populated London Borough. I sought CAT score information through FOI from all the primary schools within 1 mile of Mossbourne Academy. There were 27 such schools including two in the neighbouring borough of Islington. Six of the schools did not send any pupils to Mossbourne in September 2011. I did not seek any further information from these schools.

The Admissions Policy zones were based on the location of the home addresses of pupils not the location of the primary school they attended, so not all the pupils from the inner zone primaries lived in the inner zone and not all the pupils from the outer zone primaries lived in the outer zone.

The primary schools were generally far less co-operative with my FOI enquiries than was Mossbourne. The majority had failed to respond within the statutory 20 working day period and I only obtained full compliance after threatening formal complaints to governors and through the intervention of the Learning Trust, which went to a great deal of trouble to explain the legal status of FOI to primary school heads and to chase up their FOI responses.

The main purpose of my enquiries was to determine the extent to which the Mossbourne admission cohort from each primary differed from that of the full Y6 in terms of mean CATs scores. The results are as follows.

> Inner Zone primaries: mean Y6 CAT = 94
>
> Mean Mossbourne admitted CAT = 99
>
> Inner and Outer Zone primaries: mean Y6 CAT = 96
>
> Mean Mossbourne admitted CAT = 100

This shows that Mossbourne did indeed, on average, select more able cohorts from its local primary schools in a way that its predecessor Hackney Downs school could not. Furthermore the degree of selection of higher ability pupils was greater for the inner zone primaries than for those in the outer zone.

According to Mossbourne the numbers admitted were as follows.

> 30 inner zone pupils admitted with a mean CAT score of 99.
>
> 92 outer zone pupils admitted with a mean CAT score of 101.
>
> 15 of the outer zone pupils were from outside Hackney and these had a mean CAT score of 104.

It is quite possible that these mean CAT scores admitted according to the two sources, primary schools, and Mossbourne are in agreement because for example the discrepancy between the inner zone pupils' totals could be because a number of inner zone primary pupils in fact attend primary schools located in the outer zone and vice-versa.

The appeals information is however informative. According to Mossbourne, the 22 successful appeals had a mean CAT score of 92 (30th percentile). The 100 unsuccessful appeals were for children with a mean CAT score of 84 (14th percentile).

It seems likely that most of the 122 appeals were from inner zone families for which Mossbourne is the neighbourhood school. This is a local community characterised by extreme social deprivation resulting in high FSM. The last FSM figure for Hackney Downs school was 77 percent. Hackney Downs school, as an unbanded LA Community School, had to accept applicants on the basis of proximity. As it became progressively less popular it had to accept *all* applicants because it had surplus places.

The *Guardian* Education Editor was therefore correct in stating that Mossbourne recruits its pupils from the same severely deprived area served by Hackney Downs, However, unlike Hackney Downs, *it doesn't have to take all of them*. There were 30 places reserved for inner zone pupils in Band A. The 30 pupils that filled these places could quite possibly have been the only inner band pupils that had Band A qualifying CAT scores. If there were less than 30 then the spare places would have been filled by outer zone applicants.

According to the arguments set out in the preceding chapters of this book, the fact that many of these pupils may well also have qualified for FSM is largely irrelevant. It's cognitive ability that counts. This left 90 places in bands B, C and D. This was nowhere near enough for all the inner zone pupils with lower CAT scores because, as we_can see, 122 of those that were rejected appealed. This is a far greater number of appeals than for any other Hackney school.

As 100 of the appeals had a mean CAT score of only 84 (14th percentile) and the 22 that succeeded only 92 (30th percentile) and taking into account that most rejected applications would not have resulted in appeals at all, it is clear that, as is normally the case in areas of high social deprivation, the average neighbourhood CAT scores are very low. However *some* of these pupils *are* more able and the Mossbourne banding system makes it possible for these to be admitted to their neighbourhood school where similarly able pupils are also well represented. This would not be possible either in a selective grammar school system, or in a comprehensive system not using banded admissions regardless of whether the schools were Academies or maintained by the Local Authority.

Although its banding process is selective it is designed to produce a genuinely all-ability intake despite being geographically located in an area where less able children are hugely over-represented.

Should Mossbourne be criticised for this? Absolutely not. Mossbourne has provided an all-ability, fully comprehensive school to which its local community has access on a basis that is likely to be as fair as possible in the current circumstances of school regulation. Like all good comprehensives Mossbourne is raising the opportunities and life chances of its pupils across the full ability range.

The 1988 Education Act made it impossible for Hackney Downs school to continue to achieve this without either banded admissions (not open to LA schools at the time) or an enlightened LA like the Inner London Education Authority ILEA (abolished by the Thatcher government) willing to use its powers to balance admissions through control of catchment areas.

The prospects for the pupils rejected by Mossbourne are also improved by banding because the LA wide system introduced by the Learning Trust has resulted in all the alternative Community Schools offering genuinely all-ability comprehensive education (even if not as balanced as Mossbourne) so there are no sink schools. In Hackney, it appeared to be (at the time of writing) to be the religious schools that struggled hardest for applications from higher ability pupils.

This shows that Mossbourne can maintain its high mean intake CAT score despite recruiting from primary schools with a lower mean score, *because it is the more able pupils that are preferentially selected regardless of their possible social disadvantage.*

As schools are always likely to vary with regard to mean CAT scores and because cognitive ability is the main driver of school attainment, not relative affluence or social class, as correctly argued by Peter Saunders (1.3), it makes school league tables that take no account of such differences statistically worthless and explains why hundreds of schools serving poor communities with low average ability intakes, like Hackney Downs school, have been written off as failing when their comparatively low raw GCSE scores were just what should have been expected from their intake ability profiles. It is important to note that there is no *necessary* disadvantage to any pupils attending a lower average intake CAT score school provided their GCSE results do justice to their cognitive abilities. A school with a poorer intake ability profile could have been achieving just the same success for their more able pupils as Mossbourne, but there would be proportionately fewer of them, resulting in the league table position of the school being lower. However, the more balanced the intake ability profile, the easier it is for any comprehensive school to be able to adequately meet the developmental entitlements of all of its pupils.

So securing reasonably balanced intakes is important for any comprehensive education system, but for complete fairness they only need to be *exactly* balanced in a competitive league table based system like that which uniquely prevails in England. As we have seen even in Hackney, which probably has the fairest system currently possible, further improvements require the dismantling of school league tables together with the artificially created market that they drive.

## 4.7 Why was it impossible for Hackney Downs School to succeed?

The preceding discussion makes this obvious. To answer the question in greater depth it is necessary to consider all the reasons why Mossbourne's much maligned predecessor, Hackney Downs school, failed to survive. Was it just a very poor school that deserved to be closed under any education system? This is what Maureen O'Connor wrote in the *Independent* of 16 September 1999:

> The "market" in school places meant that as Hackney Downs declined it received such a high proportion of boys with special needs that it became, in its pupil composition, closer to a special school than even a secondary modern.
>
> Hackney Downs was a grotesque example of the market at its most vicious, making teaching and learning harder with each term. As HMI commented, there were children in the school who were beyond the remit of any normal classroom. The same market affected teacher recruitment and, by the end of its life, it was staffed almost entirely by young teachers in the first few years of their careers. Incompetent? The Education Association certainly thought some were, though the fact that most of the staff have moved on to successful careers elsewhere suggests that they were not so very different from staff in many other London schools. They were certainly inexperienced, as was the management in a school which had four headteachers in its last five years of life.

So how did it get like this and could its fate have been avoided? Let us consider a hypothetical history for Hackney Downs school, situated at the centre of an area of poor housing and social deprivation. Let us further assume that levels of affluence rise further away from the location of the school. It is not difficult to accept that deprived areas produce a higher proportion of problem pupils (C1.4, 4.8). However even the poorest areas produce some higher ability pupils and universal CAT testing can find them. The first Mossbourne Principal, Sir Michael Wilshaw, has been proved correct in his confidence that a good comprehensive school with effective teaching can overcome disadvantages that arise from relative poverty.

He has thus provided a great service to the principle of comprehensive education when much of the right wing media and most of the Conservative party are only too ready to blame comprehensive schools for declining standards. He is also right in insisting that it is much easier to provide educational opportunities across the ability range if the school *contains* the full ability range.

Let us now assume that at one time, back at the start of the league table system in the early 1990s, Hackney Downs was a popular, oversubscribed school (it does not matter for the sake of the following argument whether this is true or not). One of the reasons for such success might have been a good local record for Special Needs teaching encouraging recruitment from its immediate locality, which provided an especially rich source of such pupils.

Despite this, more affluent parents from areas of more expensive housing further away, impressed by the school's good reputation for effective teaching, were still happy to seek places at the school.

But if Hackney Downs' applications had risen to exceed the places available then the LA's oversubscription criteria would have been applied and as an LA controlled school Hackney Downs would have had no control over the effects of the LA's General Admissions Policy whose dominant provision would have been proximity to the school.

So the parents living nearest, where there were greater proportions of children with Special Needs and lower proportions of more able children, would have had priority over more affluent parents living further away, where the incidence of Special Needs was less and a greater proportion of children were more able.

Furthermore, the more over-subscribed Hackney Downs might have become, the more that less able, more local children would have filled the school, denying places to the less problematic children of more affluent parents that lived further away. It would not have taken long within the league table culture for this process to have destroyed any lingering good reputation the school may have had and for its inevitable slide down the league tables to destroy its popularity with parents.

This does not have to have been the actual history of Hackney Downs to understand that whatever policies the school had adopted it could not have avoided the fate described in the *Independent* article. League tables make it inevitable that LA schools geographically located at the centre of areas of high social deprivation with proximity based admission policies would have eventually failed to meet 'floor targets', and under the 'zero tolerance of failure' policy of New Labour, become candidates for closure and replacement by new banded Academies that could avoid admitting the problem pupils.

It is unbanded Academies located like Mossbourne in poor areas, but whose sponsors and managers believed that the invigorating effect of a commercial sponsor applying the purgative rigour of the free market would be sufficient to secure transformations, that have proved to be the least successful, especially with the demise of the 'vocational equivalent scam' (3.3, 3.4, 3.5) that appeared to provide protection, albeit to the ultimate disadvantage of their pupils,

Sir Michael Wilshaw and his co-founders of Mossbourne were therefore very wise to take the banding route to success. There is nothing unreasonable or educationally undesirable about this decision.

## 4.8 Why do areas of poor housing produce a lower proportion of brighter children?

This association is very hard for many on the political left to accept, often resulting in a 'shoot the messenger' response. Therefore the explanation has to be clearly set out.

There are many reasons on a variety of levels, none of which necessarily require any resort to explanations based on genetic inheritance.

We can start with the long established pattern that children's success at school is strongly linked to parental academic qualifications. If we make the further reasonable assumption that parents with better qualifications tend to have better jobs with higher pay and that parents that can afford it tend to move to more 'up market' areas of housing then we have a pretty convincing explanation.

A more academic argument is made by Peter Saunders (1.3) in his Civitas book, *Social Mobility Myths* (June 2010).

Far from being housing of last resort, living in a well-built council house in a pleasant suburb was a perfectly sensible lifestyle choice before the massive house price inflation caused by Margaret Thatcher's housing policies, later enthusiastically taken up by New Labour, made it an economic necessity for aspiring families to 'get onto the housing ladder' (1.4).

Poor mean cognitive ability postcodes are not however monopolised by council housing. In many northern towns the poorest housing is increasingly not council houses but privately rented (and sometimes even privately owned) Victorian terraces. Such privately rented housing was widely condemned in the 1960s as Rachmanism after the notoriously exploitive private landlord whose exposure led to rent controls that have long since been abolished.

Comprehensive education had always assumed neighbourhood schools, and enlightened LAs like the former Inner London Education Authority (ILEA) well understood the link between cognitive ability, social class and areas of deprivation. School catchment areas were devised so as to make its schools as socially heterogeneous as possible. These powers were removed by the 1988 Education Act.

## 4.9 Comparisons with Cumbria

Cumbria is an unlikely local authority to choose to compare with Hackney. Cumbria is geographically one of the largest and least densely populated Local Authorities in England. It is predominantly rural and affluent over most of its area. Hackney is one of the smallest, most densely populated, largely urban and one of the most deprived, although significant pockets of affluence certainly exist, and growing numbers of professionals appear to be moving to parts of the borough.

However what Hackney shares with Cumbria is that all of its pupils took Cognitive Ability Tests at age 10 or 11 and that I happen to possess a substantial amount of these CAT data. My Cumbria data are not recent (up to 2004) whereas my Hackney data are up to 2011. In 2004 there were 42 state funded Cumbria secondary schools whereas in 2011 Hackney had just 12. In 2004, Cumbria schools' average intake CAT score was 100, the same as Mossbourne Academy in 2011. Given that three Hackney schools do not take part in the banding process I cannot calculate the mean CAT score for Hackney. I have estimated it to be in the range 95-97.

The five lowest mean school secondary admission CAT scores in Cumbria in 2004 were, 91, 92, 94, 95 and 95. These were all schools serving poor areas in the former industrial towns of South and West Cumbria except for one that served a large and notoriously deprived council estate in the City of Carlisle. The five highest mean school CAT scores (leaving out the single Cumbria selective grammar school) were, 105, 104, 104, 104 and 102. These schools are all in affluent country towns. None of the Cumbria schools with a mean score around 100 (the Mossbourne score) served communities with any significant proportion of social deprivation.

What this shows is that although Mossbourne does indeed take a very high proportion of its pupils from poor families living in the most deprived parts of the borough, its admissions policy succeeds in selecting the most able of these while rejecting a much larger number of others of lower cognitive ability. Mossbourne therefore truly does have an intake characterised by a significant degree of social deprivation (as noted in the OfSTED report and correctly stated by the *Guardian* Education Editor). But it also has an intake *ability profile* typical of a socially and economically mixed community in an English shire county (not noted by OfSTED or mentioned by the *Guardian*).

This should not be taken to diminish the achievement of Mossbourne as a comprehensive school. Having selected a disproportionate number of bright children from its deprived neighbourhood community it is still necessary to provide the support, ethos and culture needed for these pupils to succeed. Mossbourne appears to be meeting this challenge.

## 4.10 Mossbourne's 2011 Exam Results

These show that Mossbourne operated an exemplary broad and balanced KS4 curriculum providing a wide variety of courses designed to facilitate all possible career, further and higher education requirements.

An example of the fitness for purpose of the Mossbourne curriculum could be seen in the provision of science courses. Many smaller schools lacking sufficient numbers of able pupils find it difficult to provide separate GCSE courses in biology, chemistry and physics, and offer a double award science course to meet the needs of both potential science A level students as well as for pupils not intending to take science A levels. This is a compromise that such schools have to work hard with to be completely satisfactory, but Mossbourne provided both routes.

However the rationale for the further non-GCSE double award science course taken through BTEC is more questionable.

There are many schools, especially unbanded Academies, (de

Waal 2009) that required most or all of their pupils' KS4 science experience to be through BTEC applied science and this was often through the BTEC First Diploma that was worth 4 x GCSEs (3.1). I am a former science teacher having taught KS4 science throughout my teaching career including all of my headship years. The balance of view from my continuing contacts in science teaching is that BTEC Applied Science was not a sufficient science qualification for entry into any post-16 science course nor was it likely to help gain employment in any science related industry.

This is another example of the 'vocational curriculum' route to league table success, 5+A*-C *and* the DfE Value Added measure, that New Labour introduced and which Michael Gove, to his credit finally ended from 2014. Where they remain, BTEC type courses will be worth only a single GCSE and will have to be substantially revised.

Mossbourne's dabbling in such 'vocational' curriculum was on a relatively minor scale because Mossbourne had plenty of the more able pupils needed to support the harder GCSE science courses. However, the role of Academies in general in promoting easy high scoring (for the school) 'vocational' courses was considerable (Titcombe 2008, and De Waal 2009). The latter reference to a Civitas paper shows that this organisation generally regarded as on the right of British politics was also suspicious of the Labour government's pro-Academy propaganda. It can be read and downloaded here:

www.civitas.org.uk/pdf/secrets_success_academies.pdf

## 4.11 Mossbourne's GCSE results related to its CAT ability profile

There is a problem here because I have the 2011 intake CAT profile and the 2011 GCSE results. Obviously these do not relate to the same cohort of pupils. The 2011 Y11 entered Mossbourne as Y7 in 2006. The 2011 Y13, that produced the 7 students accepted into Cambridge entered Mossbourne in 2004; the first intake in what was one of the pioneer Blair Academies. All my CAT data is from the Learning Trust and their earliest records relate to the 2007 intake. I assume therefore that 2008 was the first year that Hackney's LA wide system of CAT tests taken by all Y6 pupils in primary schools and admissions organised by the Learning Trust came into existence.

Prior to that the CAT tests were taken at Mossbourne Academy on a Saturday and at another Academy so the admissions system was then more exclusive, required more effort on the part of poor families and is therefore likely to have produced a higher ability profile. The 2013 Y11 results were for the first intake that took their CAT in primary schools administered by the Learning Trust. The %5+ A*-C figures including English and maths for the previous three years are shown as follows.

2009: 86%, 2010: 82%, 2011: 82%

Given that the comparable national figures were increasing year-on-year, and that the government, like its New Labour predecessor, regarded this as to be expected in good schools, then Mossbourne might already have been considered as 'coasting'! This is obviously ridiculous as is the notion that meaningfully real national GCSE results can have improved steadily year-on-year over the last 20 years, when the OECD/PISA international tests tell a different story (1.10, 2.5). In this Sir Michael Wilshaw and I appear to be in agreement. He is quoted in a *Guardian* article of 17 September 2011 as follows:

> Wilshaw subscribes to the view, widely held on the right of the education debate but furiously contested on the left, that standards are slipping. "Has the system made sufficient demands on our young people? Has it been sufficiently rigorous? Has it given up on academic subjects too easily? Have we gone for the soft option too often? Yes we have," he says, answering his own questions in a manner that makes him sound more like a politician than a teacher. "At 15 we're two years behind China in maths. We, as a nation, should be alarmed.

The *Guardian* was however wrong in suggesting that only those on the political right share Sir Michael's view.

### C 4.11 Hackney's Learning Trust: an example of what a local authority can do by Henry Stewart

*A post on LSN July 2011*

*Toby Young (founder of the West London Free School) challenged Local Schools Network writers to set out the conditions that academies and free schools needed to fulfil to be acceptable. It was an interesting discussion. I argued that they should be co-ordinated by their local authority, to whom they should be accountable for the quality of their education and who should organise admissions. Toby responded that he felt this was too onerous, and that his side believed schools should be able to freely compete and act in a "selfish" manner – implying that he saw local authorities as getting in the way. To explain the very positive, indeed vital, role that local authorities can play let me give the example of Hackney (where I live) and the Learning Trust.*

*Ten years ago Hackney was bottom or close to bottom nationally for its GCSE results. I know many parents who left the borough when their children were 9 or 10, to avoid Hackney's secondary schools. The phrase "our education is as bad as Hackney's" was one of the worst insults that could be thrown around in local government.*

*All that has changed. The % of 16 year olds getting 5 GCSEs (including English & maths) has gone from 26% in 2003 to 55% in 2010. Despite having the same levels of deprivation as before, the borough is now 67th (out of 167) in the country for raw GCSE results. Every single non-religious secondary school in Hackney is over-subscribed. Only last week a friend attended a meeting on secondary transition, which was full of Haringey parents trying to find out how to get their children into Hackney schools. Alan Wood, Chief Executive of the Learning Trust, has just been given a CBE in recognition of this success.*

*Note that it is the non-religious schools that are over-subscribed. In contrast all four religious schools (Jewish and Christian) have spare places. In Hackney you will not find parents suddenly starting to attend church as their children approach secondary age. Instead they will do their damnedest to get into the wide range of excellent secular secondary schools. And the Learning Trust, an independent not-for-profit body that has run Hackney's education since 2002, can be very proud of its role in achieving this.*

*For some LSN readers the Learning Trust's focus on academies is controversial. There are now five newly built academy schools in Hackney (Mossbourne, Bridge, Petchey, City and Skinners) and, with conversions, it may be that all but one of the non-religious secondaries will become Academies. But, under the last Labour government, the only way to get funding for a new school was to agree to an academy and so the Trust played the only game in town. Though the transformation is not down to the Academies. Hackney first topped the mainland England table for Contextual Value Added in 2007, before any academy had got GCSE results. And even the 2010 results include only one academy (Mossbourne).*

*I do agree with Toby that competition can be healthy. The phenomenal results of Mossbourne have been a spur to the rest of us. From Stoke Newington School (SNS), where I am Chair, we visit the other secondaries to see what we can learn – as they, in turn, visit SNS for the same reasons. But just as private sector competition works only within a regulated environment, so in local authorities the co-ordination of the local authority is crucial. To enable a system of 'fair banding' primary school students are tested. But they sit just one test which all schools use and the local authority administers admissions for all the secondaries. (Though there is a little wiggle room in the appeals, which are handled by schools.) All the schools are genuinely comprehensive with a wide range of abilities and none are seen as second-class.*

*So what is the cause of this success and what can other boroughs learn from it? I would put it down to The Learning Trust's active intervention: the high and demanding expectations, the refusal to accept excuses and the active intervention. This has meant, sometimes controversially, closing under-performing schools and moving on under-performing headteachers.*

*As a Chair I know that, if my school under-performs, the Trust will intervene with a mixture of challenge and support. And I also know, because it has happened to fellow Chairs, that if the school were to continue to under-perform then I would get a call explaining that the governors need to take action and change the leadership. I don't know how often this has happened but I would say at least a dozen heads in Hackney have been quietly moved on. This may sound tough but it is an education authority that will take whatever action is needed to ensure Hackney students get the quality of education they deserve.*

*And this is the problem with Toby Young's picture of individually competing schools, accountable only to the education minister. Will the DfE have its finger on the pulse throughout the country and be able to actively intervene in the same way? Will it spot if some schools are not doing as well as they should even if their raw scores are above average? Will it provide targeted intervention to support individual schools? Will it know when an individual school needs a change of leadership, even if the governors are reluctant to take action?*

*And will the picture that Toby paints (and that Gove presumably supports) of individual schools competing selfishly actually create the success we need? Or will it lead to many of them administering admissions to get the best possible entries for their own school, and then not co-operating (as Hackney schools now do, though they didn't in the early days of the Academies) to take their fair share of the more challenging students, and those with greater needs? Will we see all schools succeeding, as in Hackney, or will we see some schools becoming the ones that all parents want to go to, while others enter a declining spiral as they become second choice?*

*In Hackney we already have the mixture of community schools and Academies that may become the norm across the country. But we have a very active local education authority working to ensure the best education for all, and all schools working with it whatever their status. The result is that all the secondaries are successful and in high demand and that is what we surely want across the country. But it won't happen without that vital co-ordinating role of a strong local authority.*

*Perhaps it is time to learn from success, rather than diving into a new world of uncertainty and possible chaos.*

## 4.12 The Cambridge entry successes

The *Guardian* article of 18 August 2011 implies that these seven Mossbourne students are from the area, "severely hit by the riots".

According to information provided by Mossbourne in fact just two lived in the Hackney inner zone (within 1000m of Mossbourne), four lived in the outer zone (anywhere within the Borough of Hackney) and one lived outside the Borough.

The Hackney inner zone comprised a lot more than the Pembury Estate, where the 2011 Hackney riots were concentrated, so it is quite possible that none of these students came from a 'riot hit' neighbourhood.

The 2011 Mossbourne intake contained 6 pupils in the top 2 percent of the national ability range. The 2004 intake may well have contained more. That pupils of such cognitive ability at age 10 should eventually gain entry to Cambridge is therefore not that surprising provided they attended a good school that knew how to prepare them for the Cambridge admission process.

Mossbourne is a genuinely comprehensive school with the full range of ability that includes many pupils with severe learning difficulties. Mossbourne appears to eschew grand titles relating to specialisms or business. It chooses to associate itself with LA Community Schools by adopting the title, 'Community Academy', and appeared (in 2012) to be proudly part of the Hackney comprehensive system. Its success is not therefore just a credit to Mossbourne, but also to the local comprehensive system of which it is happy to be a part.

This supports Henry Stewart's claims in his LSN post (C4.11).

The fact that all seven Mossbourne students were admitted to Cambridge and none to Oxford suggests a degree of liaison between Mossbourne and one or more Cambridge Colleges that did not exist with Oxford. Again, all credit to Mossbourne and to Cambridge University.

## 4.13 What are the reasons for Mossbourne's success?

Mossbourne in 2012 was undoubtedly a well-run school with high expectations of staff and pupils and a strong commitment to intervening positively in all necessary ways that it judged to be required to support pupils' achievements. It had a very firm disciplinary system and a posh uniform. These latter factors may or may not be major contributors to the quality of learning in the school, but what is certain is that they do not depend on Academy status. Community and Religious schools also have full powers to decide their own policies in terms of pupil discipline and uniform.

Mossbourne has an expensive new building, access to special grants and more freedom to spend its money as it chooses. The modern facilities and ability to spend more on teachers, support staff and resources is certainly an advantage. Aside from this Mossbourne appears to deploy its budget much like any LA comprehensive school.

Academies can have corporate sponsors from the world of industry, finance and business. Mossbourne however is sponsored by a moderate and humane private individual, the late Sir Clive Bourne and the Bourne Family Trust.

Academies are claimed to have more freedom over the curriculum. Mossbourne's curriculum however is set up very much like a mainstream comprehensive school of the 1980s. The basic structures are divided on the basis of pastoral and curricular. The former is organised in year-based tutor teams led by Heads of Year. Curriculum organisation is on the basis of strong subject department teams led by Heads of Department, although Mossbourne has a different name for them. Each department is responsible for its own suites of teaching areas.

Academies however differ from Community comprehensives in one vital respect. They have the power to set their own Admissions Policies and it is here that a gulf of opportunity opens up that is not normally available to LA schools, which are bound by the Common Admissions Policy of the Local Authority. Religious schools have more freedoms, which many exploit with some vigour, but Academies only have to get the approval of the Secretary of State for Education for their Admission Policies and that has usually been readily forthcoming even for arrangements that may disadvantage neighbouring LA schools. The most important of these freedoms has been the right to have banded admissions policies driven by Cognitive Ability Testing. The enormous significance of this has been explained at length and in detail.

Mossbourne started life with this huge advantage over other Hackney schools, but in co-operation with the Learning Trust, has been happy to join a common admissions system ceding much of the responsibility for secondary transfer, in effect, to the Local Authority. This includes distribution of prospectuses, the co-ordinating of open evenings and communicating the process and its outcomes to parents.

Mossbourne is indeed a very good school but all its successful practices are, in principle, transferable to LA schools. In Hackney, but not elsewhere, this has included its crucial CAT based banded admissions system.

## 4.14 Objections to the Principle of Banded Admissions

The objections to banding take three forms, all of which usually come from the political left. The first is the objection in principle to any form of IQ type testing as being associated with the eugenics movement. Amongst such objectors will be those that deny the validity of the concept of 'general intelligence or cognitive ability'. I have tried to address this objection throughout this book and especially in Part 1.

The second objection is to any form of selection that inhibits the right of a parent to send their child to their nearest school. I have great sympathy with this but we are where we are in England after several decades of anti-egalitarian education legislation, the selling of council houses and the promotion of a private housing asset bubble whose collapse will not necessarily resolve the problems of demography and social polarisation that it helped to create.

This is not a good starting point for the sorts of reforms that are needed. Most European countries avoided the Thatcherite free market social experiment model endorsed and extended by New Labour, thereby largely but not entirely avoiding the creation of deprived, low cognitive ability ghettoes on the English scale.

For example, Finland, whose pupils consistently score very highly in the international PISA education standards league table, is able to operate a fairly pure form of uniform neighbourhood comprehensive schools without intake issues being a serious problem.

The third objection is that banding would encourage socially divisive streaming within schools. One London school divided itself into three separate schools on the basis of cognitive ability testing, with distinctive uniforms to identify the three pupil streams. This does not mean that CAT testing inevitably leads towards such an outcome. Peter Mortimore (2011) raises this concern as a major objection to banding that is widely shared. He states:

> Banding pupils is thus a problem because pupils, once categorised, tend to think of themselves in this way. For those placed in the top group, such an identity might further boost their confidence. But for others, labels may act as a limiting self-fulfilling prophesies.

This, however, is not primarily an argument about banding but about streaming, setting and mixed ability teaching. I have deliberately not strayed into this area in this Case Study. My central argument about Mossbourne is that as a good comprehensive school serving a socially deprived community, its banded admissions system gives it a pupil ability profile that enables its success, wherever its pedagogy falls on the mixed ability-setting-streaming spectrum.

Many observers ignorant of the powerful consequences of banded admissions systems have attributed Mossbourne's success directly to its disciplinary and uniform arrangements. Such assumptions generally accord with the educational mindset of the political right, while more liberally inclined parents and educationalists may be discomforted by such authoritarianism. There are certainly parents in Hackney that rule out Mossbourne for this reason.

The key point here is that the evidence about mixed ability teaching is inconclusive, with plenty of research and a seemingly limitless range of dubious anecdotes to provide succour to both sides of the argument.

What is certain is that without banding Mossbourne could not succeed in the current system whatever pedagogic strategies were used. Mossbourne is adamant that it does not use CAT scores to stream or set its pupils and it does not disclose them to pupils or parents. It is doubtful whether this non-disclosure policy could survive a Data Protection Act enquiry by a parent, however, it is clear that Mortimore's 'fulfilling expectations' arguments are independent of CAT based banded admissions systems. There would be nothing to stop a banded Hackney school adopting a full universal mixed ability teaching model. Indeed banding would be necessary for such a model to have any chance of success because without it, it would be impossible to guarantee the genuinely mixed ability classes needed for such a system to fulfill its potential.

## 4.15 The *Guardian* Articles

It is appropriate to end this case study where we started, with the article co-authored by the then *Guardian* Education Editor, Jeevan Vasagar on 18 August 2011. This appears to make a number of assumptions:

*That Mossbourne has a similar intake to its predecessor, Hackney Downs school.*

It hasn't. Mossbourne's intake typically has had an average cognitive ability of 100, the national average, whereas Hackney Downs' was likely to have been around 84, similar to the 100 pupils refused admission to Mossbourne and whose appeals were turned down. 84 represents the 14th percentile, meaning that only the lowest 14 percent of the national population had a cognitive ability lower than the average cognitive ability of the Hackney Downs pupils. Not only is Mossbourne's intake massively more able than that of its predecessor, it is significantly more able than the Hackney average and that of many of the other secondary schools that participate in the same system of banded admissions.

*The school's success does not depend on its selective intake.*

It most certainly does. Mossbourne selects on cognitive ability regardless of social deprivation. Mossbourne attempted to admit 60 percent of its pupils from within 1000m of the school, an area of severe social deprivation, but it selected only a small proportion of the pupils that live there. Large numbers of those with lower CAT scores are rejected. In other words the socially deprived surroundings of Mossbourne Academy produce children with a much lower than average cognitive ability (but still covering the full range) from which Mossbourne selects an intake whose cognitive ability (but not social or economic profile) matches the national profile.

*That Sir Michael Wilshaw's assertions in terms of low-income homes, FSM entitlement and bilingualism are more relevant than the CAT score profile he declines to mention.*

They are not. It is cognitive ability that counts. The *Guardian* articles fail to make any reference to admissions issues like CAT scores and banding that lie at the core of Mossbourne's success. But then all the print and broadcast media are guilty of the same omission. Less defensibly, this is also true of OfSTED reports. Hopefully this will now change with Sir Michael as the new head of OfSTED.

*That the seven students admitted to Cambridge University in 2011 come from deprived backgrounds.*

One of the seven does not come from Hackney at all and a further four are from Mossbourne's outer-zone, which is anywhere in Hackney further than 1000m from the school. Again the incorrect assumption appears to be that it is mainly the social and/or ethnic background that restricts access to top universities rather than cognitive ability. Mossbourne's intake exactly reflects the national average in terms of cognitive ability so, while highly creditable, it is not unduly remarkable that a tiny proportion might progress to

Oxford or Cambridge especially if the school has established good links with those university's admission systems.

In the last week of 2011 Sir Michael, the new OfSTED chief designate, hinted that he had indeed learned much from his Mossbourne experience. With surely a tacit acknowledgement to his former school's active support and co-operation with the Hackney Learning Trust, Sir Michael was reported as follows in the *Guardian* of 28 December.

### New Ofsted chief proposes creation of team to identify failing Academies

Sir Michael Wilshaw, the incoming head of Ofsted, has proposed the creation of a team of local commissioners to identify failing Academies.

A team of local commissioners should be employed to identify institutions that should lose their academy status and find headteachers who should be replaced, the incoming head of Ofsted has said.

As more schools become independent Academies, Sir Michael Wilshaw called for the creation of the network of commissioners who would report back on the performance of schools in their area.

In other words quite a lot of Academies were increasingly being recognised to be failing despite their free market pedigree. Sir Michael appeared to be suggesting the need for the equivalent of something like Local Education Authorities to be set up on the model of the Hackney Learning Trust. That this should be necessary suggests an acknowledgement that the many hundreds of pseudo-independent Academy Conversions and Free Schools that Michael Gove created cannot be effectively regulated from the centre and that local intervention and support is needed if Mossbourne's success is to be replicated.

In this respect he appears to share the view of London Mayor Boris Johnson, and they are both surely correct.

The model of most of the nation's schools being centrally funded, managed, and regulated by the Department for Education, operating under the direct political control of the Secretary of State is not just fundamentally authoritarian and profoundly anti-democratic, but is likely to fail under the sheer size and complexity of the bureaucracy involved, not to mention its enormous cost.

These strains were increasingly emerging throughout 2014 as this book was being prepared for publication.

*Part 5*

*What is 'Good Education' and how is it different?*

## 5.1 Some history of grading revisited

In 2.1 I introduced our fictional pupils Janet and John and explored how their school curriculum experiences might have come to be so different. To more fully explain this we have to return to (1.10) and the history of the English examination system.

The direct ancestors of GCSE, GCE and CSE, were historically graded in accordance with the principles of Bloom's Taxonomy (1.7), with the C grade (CSE Grade 1) requiring significant performance at the first stage of 'higher order thinking' or above. This has its roots in the role of the GCE in matriculation (qualifying) for university entrance purposes (1.10). One of the most respected GCE examining boards was NUJMB (Northern Universities Joint Matriculation Board), a public body. GCSE Grades D to G were designed to cover and discriminate between all the lower levels above U (unclassified). This was necessary because at the other end of the scale A Levels were regarded as being a 'gold standard'; by definition entirely within Bloom higher order thinking, with success leading to university degree courses that assumed and developed further proficiency and applications within these highest levels. The GCSE C grade had its origins as the crucial gateway step on the ladder to higher order cognitive attainment and was therefore required to be an educationally sound threshold for progressing onto A Level courses.

This rational and soundly based foundation could have been consolidated and refined by the government's persisting with National Curriculum Levels through Key Stage Four (KS4) as originally proposed by the National Curriculum Council. Instead, a rigorous Levels based approach to grading was abandoned in the face of the inability of a very high proportion of 'socially and economically disadvantaged' (i.e. largely working class) pupils to achieve the higher levels despite the number of imposed initiatives or the vast amount of money spent by New Labour on the problem. It became more attractive for New Labour to point to the newly acquired League Table success of previously 'underperforming' schools as evidence that attainment had been successfully raised as a result of its policies, than to address the fact of low cognitive ability patterns that characterised poor communities. The illusion of school improvement brought about by fiddling the exam system was so skilfully presented that it became largely accepted as a fact by all political parties and the national news media (3.1).

## 5.2 Cognitive Acceleration – The Contribution of Philip Adey and Michael Shayer

Most teachers appear to be able to sail through their careers without much concern for, or knowledge of learning theory at all. This was also true for me until I was lucky enough to be seconded for a year onto the Master of Educational Studies Course (M. Ed.) at Leicester University in 1981.

Here alongside studying theories of learning, assessment and evaluation and the beginnings of the applications of computers in education, I carried out some educational research which was heavily influenced by the work of Michael Shayer and Philip Adey (1.5).

These educationalists progressed to Kings College, London where they set up and developed a programme of teaching for enhancing cognitive development based mainly on the learning theories of Jean Piaget. My M. Ed. dissertation was a piece of research on the practicability of matching the cognitive demand of the curriculum to the level of cognitive development of individual pupils. This is a much more sophisticated issue than streaming or setting. The basis of my work was Shayer and Adey's *Towards a Science of Science Teaching* (1981).

In *Learning Intelligence* (2002), Shayer and Adey set out six principles on which their Cognitive Acceleration pedagogy is based. The following is my understanding of these.

### Schema (plural Schemata) Theory

Schemata are general ways of thinking that apply in many parallel contexts. For example, Inhelder and Piaget (1958) famously identified the schemata of 'Formal Operations' (e.g. control of variables and formal mental modelling) that differed from the schemata characterising the previous stage of 'Concrete Operations' (e.g. simple classification and various conservations). In maths the schemata of 'Formal Operations' might be transposed to include ratio and proportion, and ability to think in terms of *variables* rather than just whole numbers'. Recognition of schemata is necessary in order to construct appropriate learning and assessment scenarios.

## Concrete Preparation

Like buildings, learning needs concrete foundations. Given that the objective is to facilitate progression to formal thinking it must be expected that individual pupils are likely to be at different cognitive stages. If the ground is to be successfully prepared for what is later to be presented then this must be founded on common language and examples from the concrete stage, that all can share and understand.

## Cognitive Conflict

Exposing pupils to cognitive conflict is central to all teaching for cognitive development. It essentially comprises presenting pupils with factual evidence that doesn't consciously or unconsciously make initial sense to them, so creating a state of discomforting mental tension. In order for the conflict to be resolved within the mind of the individual learner then a personal conceptual breakthrough is necessary. Cognitive development arises from the accumulation of such conceptual breakthroughs. If the cognitive conflict is too great then the learner might 'close down' and withdraw co-operation with the lesson. This could be at a conscious or subconscious level. Hostility to the whole subject area is therefore a possible consequence so highly skilled teaching and managing of learning is essential to avoid such an outcome. If there is insufficient cognitive conflict then the learner will just assimilate experiences at a shallow level and there will be no conceptual or cognitive gain. The work of the Russian learning theorist Vygotsky can provide a structure to help the teacher plan learning, through his 'Zone of Proximal Development' (ZPD) (1978). The ZPD is the level of cognitive challenge beyond which the learner cannot manage unaided, but not beyond what can be understood with the assistance of a teacher or more able peers. The teacher and peer group members can assist in a variety of ways that involve discussion (peers) and skillfully constructed leading questions (teacher). This is a key role of the teacher. It is only by experiencing this type of teaching and subsequently discussing it in departmental teams that the necessary teaching expertise can be built.

## Social Construction

Vygotsky (1978) asserts that understanding first appears in the social space that learners share. Only then does it become internalised by individuals. Piaget shares this view but expresses it differently. The key point is that in a school the resolution of cognitive conflict in an individual learner is normally a social process. The participants assist *each other* in grappling with the cognitive conflict. This requires a certain quality in the social relationships in the classroom. I was lucky enough early in my career to work in a school where such quality relationships existed, and it became a career goal to eventually achieve it in my headship school. Pupils have to trust and not fear the teacher if they are to risk revealing the true depth of their misunderstanding! University Challenge question master Jeremy Paxman famously might need some practice in this. Peer relationships have to be good enough for all group members to be comfortable with revealing their lack of understanding to each other as well as both collectively and individually to the teacher. This is a big ask, not to be underestimated. A school culture of behaviourist authoritarianism will not provide sufficient personal psychological security for the teacher or the pupils for the necessary social interactions to ignite. Obviously nothing can be achieved where informality degenerates into anarchy and chaos reigns. Once again great demands are placed on the teacher, who needs the skills to be able to promote positive self-sustaining, reasoned discussion between pupils. This is very difficult to achieve and the true hallmark of a good teacher. There are regrettably a growing number of schools, many judged as successful in league table terms, where relationships between school managers and teachers, teachers and pupils and pupils with peers are so limited in depth and quality that this type of high level learning is likely to be impossible.

## Metacognition

This means being aware of your own thinking process. It implies that language provides the tools for thought and that learners benefit by silently but consciously 'talking to themselves' as well as talking to peers and the teacher. The idea is that as learners experience cognitive development they also develop a metacognitive ability that can be characterised as a higher level thinking skill in itself. This links to Bloom's taxonomy (1.7, 5.7).

## Bridging

This is applying new understanding to other contexts. It could be called 'lateral thinking'. Pupils need to be encouraged to see links with other subjects and disciplines. Such activity is clearly linked to

'Creating', 'Synthesising' and 'Evaluating' that characterise the top two Bloom levels.

The difference between cognitively developmental teaching and the cramming needed to get Level 4 in SATs and Grade 'C' at GCSE maths in the school context of high stakes league tables could not be clearer. GNVQs and their 'vocational' successors did not even rise to levels that need cramming, being based largely on the 'collection' of a sufficient number of statements (assessed by tick boxes) that the students have encountered situations broadly related to the title of the course; no deep understanding being required or tested (1.11).

The teaching methods that are taking over our schools and which teachers are now increasingly compelled to adopt within the league table driven, competitive English education system, are the polar opposite of teaching for such cognitive growth. It would now be increasingly rare to find any pupils in English schools that have experienced lessons that have really stretched the students and even harder to find teachers encouraged by their 'Executive Principals' to teach in this way.

If cramming and repetition reinforced by rewards and the shame of failure have any effect at all on individual cognition then it is cognitive depression leading to rejection of challenging concepts and alienation.

These two opposing approaches are rooted in two classic alternative theoretical models of learning (1.8). Cognitive Acceleration is rooted within the 'developmental' school that emphasises the importance of challenging and refining the individual mental models (schemata) held by learners, whereas the latter comes directly from the behaviourism of B F Skinner (1.8), who believed that all learning was acquired as a result of conditioning resulting from rewarding correct responses. Think rats, dogs or pigeons in cages. Despite the fact that the behaviourist position has been largely discredited and abandoned by learning theoreticians, it corresponds more closely to the 'common sense' model usually held by the public, and regrettably the politicians in charge of our education system that should know better or at least be better advised. Note that lessons that 'cognitively accelerate' require pupils to be confronted with cognitive problems 'just above' the level at which they can solve them without assistance using their existing mental models. Teachers are now often taught never to allow children to fail to solve problems because this reinforces failure (clearly the behaviourist model), whereas for cognitive growth children need to learn in a culture that supports and encourages learning from mistakes.

Cognitive Acceleration is just one example of a teaching and learning strategy designed to secure cognitive development and Shayer and Adey represent just one such approach, albeit a very important one with proven effectiveness. In 1993 Michael Shayer and Mundher Adhami also commenced work on doing the same thing for secondary maths (CAME). The success of such teaching creates challenges for the entire curriculum and the way it is assessed and graded through the GCSE. There may well be many other effective developmental approaches in existence, and I will later refer to some that I am aware of.

Shayer and Adey's CA model is based on discrete highly structured lessons. In my headship school we used CASE (1.8) and found it to be effective not just in raising pupil performance in science, but generally, as claimed, across the curriculum. Cognitively demanding teaching that involves the recognition, nurturing and normalising of 'cognitive dissonance' on the part of pupils was also found to be highly motivating, but only if there is a learning culture where pupils expect to make mistakes and are comfortable with exploring ideas that lead nowhere as well as those that turn out to be productive.

I am proposing a definition of effective schools as those where teachers operate in collegiate professional teams, independent of government political interference, focused on securing cognitive development as an essential teaching and learning objective.

## C 5.2 High UK child death rates and neuromyths

*While the approaches of 'Cognitive Acceleration' has a proven track record of improving students' learning and achievement, many other strategies that sound like they're to do with cognition are no such thing. This is particularly the case with lessons and approaches based upon specious brain research. On 3rd May 2014 the Guardian featured an article by Sarah Boseley entitled: "UK child death rate among worst in western Europe, say experts".*

*The article was based on a report in The Lancet and made the point that children in the UK were more likely to die before they reach their fifth birthday in 2012 than in any other western European country except Malta.*

*Almost five in every 1,000 children born in the UK die before the age of five, a rate the authors of the global study said was surprising for a country with free, universal healthcare. Researchers at the Institute of Health Metrics and Evaluation (IHME) in Seattle said that 3,000 children in the UK died before their first birthday in 2012.*

*Experts said poverty and deprivation in the UK, together with cuts in welfare, were directly linked to the deaths of the youngest children. Babies who die under age of one tend to be from deprived households, have a low birth weight and have parents who smoked. Between ages of one and five, deaths are mostly linked to injuries, accidents and serious diseases such as cancer."*

*This is truly shocking, but are these data being used to falsely support links between childhood deprivation and the denial of potential for intellectual development?*

*This was the subject an equally important and compelling Guardian article the previous Saturday, 26 April 2014 by Zoe Williams entitled, "Is misused neuroscience defining early years and child protection policy?" She states: "The idea that a child's brain is irrevocably shaped in the first three years increasingly drives government policy on adoption and early childhood intervention. But does the science stand up to scrutiny?"*

*Graham Allen and Iain Duncan Smith in their 2010 collaboration wrote: "Neuroscience can now explain why early conditions are so crucial. The more positive stimuli a baby is given, the more brain cells and synapses it will be able to develop."*

*I argue in this book that 'general intelligence' is a valid and useful concept but like Shayer and Adey (1.5) I believe it to be plastic (1.4), and susceptible to development through schooling through developmental methods like those set out by these authors and researchers in their 'Cognitive Acceleration' teaching programmes (5.2) described in their 2002 book Learning Intelligence.*

*If Shayer and Adey are right, and I believe they are, then such developmental potential applies to all children including those born into deprived backgrounds. If a child's brain is indeed 'irrevocably shaped' in the first three years of life then schooling won't have much impact and spending a lot of taxpayer's money on it will be in vain.*

*Zoe Williams' article is more concerned with the implications of this assumption for social policies on adoption and early years intervention, but there are also profound implications for education.*

*This relates to my study of Mossbourne Academy (Part 4). If the neuroscience is right then Mossbourne's excellent exam results and progression to university of children from severely deprived homes (4.14) shouldn't be happening, because "impaired synapse connectivity" in early years should trump any later pedagogic intervention and limit educational attainment. Mossbourne very importantly shows that it doesn't have to. It isn't just Mossbourne that shows it to be faulty, it is also the definite evidence that at 5 to 7, and again at 11 to 13, plasticity is great enough to compensate for earlier impairments.*

*Zoe Williams suggests that 'neuroscience' may be bad science. She asks, "What if the constant references to 'brain scans of neglected children' actually just meant one brain scan, from one highly contested study? What if synaptic development were a bit more complicated than 'the more synapses the better', and what if MRI scans tell us much less than we think?"*

*This is obviously not to deny the severity of damage to young children caused by gross physical abuse, trauma and neglect, nor does it provide any comfort for the shame of the way UK children have become so undervalued and under-cared-for.*

*Bad Education (Adey, P., Dillon J., 2012) has a chapter by Corinne Read and Mike Anderson that makes the same arguments which they describe as 'neuro-myth'. They say, "we tackle the question of why neuroscience is so alluring for educators and discuss the dangers of taking a too brain-centric view of education".*

*This made me think about a possible analogy with computers. Back in the early 1980s we bought an 'Acorn Electron' for our children (at vast cost at today's prices). This was based on the famous BBC microcomputer that for a few years completely swamped all schools. We bought a 'chess program' for the Electron. This came recorded on an audio cassette and was loaded onto the computer through the headphone socket of an audio-cassette player. This chess playing software worked on the 16K RAM Electron and gave a surprisingly good game.*

*I wrote this book on a modern laptop computer whose number of processing 'synapses' and memory store are millions of time greater than those of the Electron. It is possible to purchase 'emulator' software to make modern computers think they are 16K Acorn machines and run Acorn software including our chess game.*

*However vastly increased processing power doesn't make a jot difference to the ability of the Acorn chess programme to win its games.*

*It is software not hardware that matters. As for computers, so for the minds of children. The developmental teaching methods advocated by Shayer and Adey, based on Piaget and Vygotsky (1.8) are about enabling Kahneman's System 2 cognitive ability (5.5) to develop increasing levels of sophistication, so enabling understanding that requires deeper concepts. I don't think it has so much to do with the number of synapses in the brain as with the information that passes between them and how this is processed in the biological medium.*

*What would happen if you placed an Acorn Electron and a modern laptop in an MRI scanner and played the Acorn chess programme on both? What would you learn from which 'chips' or parts of chips or memory boards lit up?*

*The fact is that despite all the developments in neurobiology and ever increasing knowledge of which bits of brains light up in MRI scanners when you are thinking different thoughts, we know virtually nothing about the physical processes directly related to the simplest levels of cognition, let alone the enduring mystery of consciousness. It is these latter that are the true currency of education and learning.*

*We should be very sceptical of neuroscience applied to the classroom.*

## 5.3 The Work of Mortimer and Scott – Leeds University

Shayer and Adey are far from alone in researching developmental approaches for enhancing understanding. They were involved with research at Leeds University in connection with the Children's Learning in Science Project (CLIS). Eduardo Mortimer and Phillip Scott have focussed on the importance of language and talking about science in classrooms for the promotion of higher levels of thinking and understanding. Like Shayer and Adey, they base much of their theoretical approach on the work of Vygotsky. The emphasis is different but all the basic themes of Shayer and Adey's cognitive acceleration approach are present as described in their 2003 book, *Meaning Making in Secondary Science Classrooms*.

While *Schema Theory* is not referred to as such, CLIS clearly recognises that the development of children's personal mental models is key to the understanding of mentally challenging ideas in science, although CLIS emphasises Vygotskian social learning rather more than Piagetian stages.

*Concrete Preparation* is approached by CLIS more in terms of the language used, as in their concept of a 'teaching spiral' starting from the concrete language of 'places' to the increasingly abstract language needed for 'things', 'essential things' and 'scientific proof for the essential things'.

It is in respect of *Cognitive Conflict* and *Social Construction* that CLIS extends the ideas of Shayer and Adey in ways that seem to me to be to be especially positive and illuminating. This is where the nature of pupil and teacher talk, with particular reference to the language used and the style of communication, is addressed in great depth and where much experimental and observational work has been done. However, there is much in the Cognitive Acceleration lesson structures that resonate with the classroom work and recommendations of Mortimer and Scott, including specific reference to 'scaffolding' on the part of the teacher in promoting positive discourse.

*Metacognition* is also clearly recognised within CLIS. For example in Chapter 2 of *Meaning Making in Secondary Science Classrooms*, we find:

> What is involved, for each participant, is an ongoing process of comparing their own understandings with the ideas that are being rehearsed on the social plane", and, "the process of internalisation always involves working on ideas, it always involves an individual meaning making step.

Such 'internalisation' implies a degree of metacognition on the part of the learner.

*Bridging,* in the sense of moving from the particular to the general is uncontroversial, but still very important for the teaching of almost everything and forms level 3 of the Bloom taxonomy. A CLIS approach is to give out sets of cards describing general scenarios relevant to the topic studied, with pupils asked to predict outcomes based on acquired knowledge and understanding. For example, pupils could be asked to consider the likelihood of corrosion being a problem in various scenarios not previously mentioned in the preceding lessons. This is a very direct approach to bridging.

Given the degree of overlap in their approaches it is perhaps surprising to find no references to Shayer, Adey or Cognitive Acceleration in 'Meaning Making in Secondary Science Classrooms'. However regardless of the scope for debate about the details there is no argument that Mortimer and Scott are just as far as Shayer and Adey from the behaviourism of Skinner that is increasingly dominating English classrooms.

## 5.4 Developing Mathematical Resilience – University of Warwick and the Open University

The following quote from the 2010 paper with this title by Sue Johnston-Wilder (Warwick University) and Clare Lee (Open University) (3.6) serves to describe their important work on maths education, the failures of which are a major thread running through this book. This is a further quote from their 2010 BERA paper http://oro.open.ac.uk/24261/2/3C23606C.pdf

> Mathematical resilience describes that quality by which some learners approach mathematics with confidence, persistence and a willingness to discuss, reflect and research. All learning

requires resilience; however, we contend that the resilience required for learning mathematics is a particular construct as a consequence of various factors including: the type of teaching often used, the nature of mathematics itself and pervasive beliefs about mathematical ability being 'fixed'.

Here we find an approach emphasising; confidence, persistence and a willingness to discuss, reflect and research.

We are clearly in the territory of Shayer, Adey, Mortimer & Scott, not to mention Part 1 of this book about the plasticity of intelligence (1.4).

The more that we studied stories from people who exhibit mathematics phobia, and read the related literature, the more that it appeared to us that the way that mathematics is often taught in English mathematics classrooms is an unwitting form of cognitive abuse. Instances of ways of working that seem calculated to cause anxiety are asking learners to perform tasks that require feats of memory at a rapid rate or to memorise formulae without understanding in classrooms where the mathematics is divorced from the reality that it models so powerfully. These ways of working have been shown by many researchers (e.g.**Boaler 2009, Jain & Dowson, 2009 and Baloglu & Koçak, 2006** ) to cause anxiety. Acting in such a way that many people are made to feel anxious, concerned or fearful seems to us to be acting in an abusive way.

Although it has frequently been in my mind I have refrained from using the term 'cognitive abuse' but this is a truly appropriate description of what I describe in Part 2. Johnston-Wilder and Lee are providing powerful support for my arguments. The 'abusive' ways of working they describe are clearly drawn from the pedagogy of behaviourism (1.8):

The literature, for example Sfard, (2008) and Lee (2006), indicates that pupils must articulate their mathematical ideas in order to effectively learn mathematics. It seems that placing pupils in the position of having to communicate what they are learning is at the core of increasing both the pupils' resilience and their thinking and learning. Sfard (2008) is clear that learning and communicating are intricately intertwined. The current mathematical culture in the school was resistant to pupil articulation with a heavy emphasis on teacher exposition and little opportunity for pupils to express their emergent understanding or misunderstandings.

After consideration, we chose to use the medium of short videos to prompt pupils to articulate their ideas. We asked a class of Year 9 pupils, aged 13 and 14 years, to collaborate in making their own videos to explain some mathematical ideas that they had recently been working on. Socio-cultural theorists (e.g. Vygotsky 1981) suggest that pupils learn from working collaboratively to build knowledge. Asking the pupils to make a video provided clear roles for each member of the group and we believed would provide motivation for the pupils to articulate their explanations in a clear and concise way.

Johnston-Wilder and Lee are clearly working in the same theoretical domain espoused by Shayer, Adey, Mortimer and Scott and once again the educational ideas of Vygotsky are dominant. What their paper does not discuss, however, is the extent to which the authors feel that 'mathematical resilience' is a general cognitive gain, transferable to other subjects and contexts, in the way that Shayer and Adey claim for 'cognitive acceleration'.

A private email exchange with Sue Johnston-Wilder on 26 June 2012, however, confirmed that she does indeed share that view.

## 5.5 Guy Claxton - more on learning resilience and developing learning capacity

Johnston-Wilder and Lee have been heavily influenced in their development of the concept of mathematical resilience by the work of Guy Claxton, who has created a major educational movement around the concept of 'learning capacity'. This has involved a sophisticated and detailed consideration and analysis of many of the strands identified as 'good learning' in this book. An enormous amount of material is available in Guy Claxton's books supported by linked websites. The following is my attempt to identify the key features of Claxton's educational movement and link them to the appropriate sections of my own analysis of what is wrong with the English education system and how more effective learning should best be promoted in our schools.

Claxton too rejects 'fixed intelligence' and believes that particular pedagogic approaches can promote what he calls 'capacity for learning'. I would argue that 'capacity for learning' is closely related to what Shayer and Adey call 'plastic intelligence'. The approaches advocated by Claxton, Shayer and Adey are entirely contrary to those of the resurgent behaviourism that are becoming increasingly dominant in our schools as a result of the perverse incentives generated by marketisation. Claxton uses a different language to that of Shayer and Adey but the links to their 'Cognitive Acceleration' work are strong. Claxton is making an important contribution to combating 'bad education' in our schools and I cannot do him justice in this short section. However I will make a start by setting out what I see to be the main principles needed for

'Developing Learning Capacity'. Much of the following is from his 2006 keynote opening address to the British Educational Research (BERA) conference at the University of Warwick. This can be read and downloaded here: _www.tloltd.co.uk/guyclaxton.php_

In this various researchers are reported as commenting as follows:

> ...traditional mathematics teaching, effective at getting those vital Cs at GCSE, leave in students' minds no discernable residue of real world utility.

> It is academically successful girls that are most likely to go to pieces when confronted by something they do not know how to do. They will get good school results but, at the same time, their learning resilience can be wafer thin.

> You can get good results in the arcane world of educational standards and still lack resilience, resourcefulness, and the ability to organise and evaluate your own learning.

And this is just about 'bright' children that are successful in the current system. What about the children that feature in Part 2 of this book? What about those rejected by the 'C grade driven', OfSTED-fearing culture of our schools (2.1)? Many teachers will recognise the pupil whose morale and sense of worth is repeatedly frustrated by perceived failure to 'get things right' and whose response is to give up, screw their work into a ball and angrily toss it aside before once again starting from the beginning. Claxton is right about the importance of 'learning capacity' and 'learning resilience'. He addresses it through the resurrection of the concept of 'Metacognition', one of the fundamental planks of Shayer and Adey's Cognitive Acceleration (5.2).

> I think we must reclaim the language of 'character' [from its Victorian public school connotations that influenced the grammar schools], and not be afraid of the value judgements that go along with it."
> "I can offer you two brand new phrases that say the same thing. They are 'epistemic mentality' and 'epistemic identity'. By 'epistemic' I mean to do with 'thinking', 'knowing' and 'learning'.

The important point being made here is that the culture of classrooms and quality of relationships affects the 'disposition' of learners and is just as important as the knowledge delivery skills of the teacher. In fact, for the promotion of 'learning capacity', it is more important. Here again the current trend in our schools appears to be in the wrong direction. The development of metacognition in pupils, meaning to be aware of one's own thinking, knowing and learning, would not appear to be readily promoted by a culture of 'zero tolerance' discipline (C2.6).

Claxton includes metacognition, within his 'epistemic mentality', referring to the whole interrelated repertoire of learning-related habits of mind that he identifies. It is the prerequisite for sharing one's personal schemata (5.2) and constructs with those of the teacher and just as importantly, with other pupils. Now we are in the territory of Mortimer and Scott (5.3) that emphasises the importance of 'pupil talk', starting with to oneself and then with others in sharing, testing and developing personal constructs. Once again a culture of 'zero tolerance' punishment tariff driven discipline is unlikely to be fertile soil for this approach to learning.

> The Cognitive Acceleration in science and maths programmes devised by Philip Adey and Michael Shayer (5.2) have consistently produced evidence of spontaneous transfer to other subjects, but again, only after the kind of extended interventions that might be expected to develop dispositions as well as skills.

Quite so. CA is all about developing positive learning 'dispositions' and hence Claxton's 'capacity for learning'.

> The classroom should be a place where talk about the process of learning, the nature of oneself as a learner, is continual and natural...The teacher challenges the learner to think about their own learning process...

What is quite clear is that the behaviourism that is increasingly being forced upon schools by the results focussed, target-driven managerialism characterised by much of the Academy and Free School culture is the polar opposite of the school culture advocated by Claxton. There is a high level of congruence between Claxton's 'Learning Capability', Shayer and Adey's 'Cognitive Acceleration' (5.2), Mortimer and Scott's 'More talk needed' (5.3), Johnston-Wilder and Lee's 'Mathematical resilience'(5.4) and Kahneman's 'Slow Thinking' (5.6). Also were he alive today Richard Dawes (5.8) would surely also be enthusiastically nodding his head.

Claxton also likes the idea of the availability of 'Wild Topics', not related to linear exam syllabuses, as promoters of learning capability. This is what the 'Leicestershire Modular Framework' (5.7) was about. The language and terminology is different but the pedagogy is the same.

Why then, with so much convergence about how to improve our schools from teachers and academia, including the odd polemicist like me, is the direction of travel of the development of the English education system so firmly in the wrong direction?

## C 5.5 Neither skills nor knowledge

I amused my eight year old granddaughter with this conundrum that I remembered from my childhood:

'Think of a number between 1 and 10 (but don't tell me what it is).
Double it.
Add 6
Halve it
Take away the number you first thought of.
The answer is 3 isn't it?'

As expected, the response was, "Wow granddad, how did you know that?"

When she repeated the exercise with different starting numbers she soon discovered that the answer was always 3, so she then asked me why this was the case.

I then gave her a much simpler conundrum.

'Think of a number'.
Add 1.
Take away the number you first thought of.
What's the answer ?"

She immediately saw that not only it was 1 but that it would always be 1, whatever number you started with. She also realised that this was the same sort of problem as the first one. She was able to generalise why both examples worked but was unable to abstract.

So is this conundrum a matter of knowledge or skills? Clearly it is neither. There was no knowledge deficit that stopped her understanding why the conundrum always worked. There was no skills deficit either. She could add, multiply, divide and subtract perfectly well.

I see this as confirmation of Piagetian developmental stages. My granddaughter is well established within the concrete stage. She can't be expected to understand in general how such conundrums work until she begins the transition to the formal stage. I would place this conundrum firmly on the border between concrete and formal. A well-established formal thinker would explain the conundrum by resorting to simple algebra. She can easily understand it as a concrete problem as in the second example but cannot generalise how it works in abstract terms.

My argument is that the primary focus of all children's education should be helping children progress through the Piagetian stages starting with consolidation of the one they are in. In Y7 most pupils will have established themselves within the concrete stage with varying degrees of confidence. KS3 and KS4 should be all about promoting development through the stages, with special reference to the concrete/formal transition that is *essential (or used to be) for accessing higher level GCSE grades and progression to A level.*

*The power of Piagetian stage theory that underpins its relevance to curriculum and teaching methods is that it doesn't matter in which subject context the child develops fastest because the cognitive gains transfer across to all subjects, all learning and all problem solving. Therefore schools can exploit children's enthusiasm for their 'favourite subject' to the benefit of deeper understanding in all subjects.*

*This is the basis of Shayer and Adey's 'Cognitive Acceleration through Science Education' (CASE) programme, which I have direct experience of. The same principles underpin CAME (Cognitive Acceleration through Maths Education) and other applications in the humanities. The approach also transfers into pre-school and infant teaching where the key transition is from pre-concrete to concrete, which is mainly about understanding various conservations.*

*All this is explained with examples from various teachers and schools in their book, Learning Intelligence (Adey, P. Shayer, M., 2002).*

*However the real brilliance of Shayer and Adey that has still not brought the deserved degree of recognition, is to combine the stage theory of Piaget with the 'social learning' theories of Vygotsky. This synthesis is central to their 'Cognitive Acceleration' strategies across the curriculum and age range.*

## 5.6 Thinking, Fast and Slow

This is the title of the 2011 book by the Nobel Laureate Daniel Kahneman, who is a cognitive psychologist at Princeton University and Emeritus Professor of Public Affairs at Woodrow Wilson School of Public and International Affairs. He was awarded the Nobel Prize in Economics in 2002. He appears to have no background in learning theory or pedagogy and his book makes no direct reference to school age education or curriculum, so what is the relevance to the failures of the English education system?

It is because all his work is based on his assertion that humans have two discrete modes of thinking that he refers to as System 1 and System 2. System 1 is a result of human evolution and to a major extent is written into the human genome. It is the 'fast thinking' that is linked to survival in evolutionary terms. It is very good at solving certain kinds of problems very rapidly but frequently fails spectacularly with complex problems associated with scientific and mathematical concepts that millions of years of evolution have not prepared us for, other than giving us large brains with a highly flexible cerebral cortex. Kahneman describes System 1 as "a machine for jumping to conclusions", which is the title of Chapter 7 in his book.

This is precisely the theme of Lewis Wolpert's *The Unnatural Nature of Science* (1992). Kahneman would surely agree with the former 1997 Economics Laureate James Meade (1.6) about the limitations and dangers of common sense.

I first came across Daniel Kahneman by accident on listening to BBC Radio 4 in June 2012, when he was being interviewed about his new book. He repeated the following puzzle and the programme presenter asked the audience to phone in their solutions.

> A bat and ball costs £1.10 in total.
>
> The bat costs one pound more than the ball.
>
> How much does the ball cost?

System 1 provides the almost instant answer of 10p, which is, of course incorrect. The correct solution requires the conscious slow thinking of the cerebral cortex that Kahneman refers to as System 2. Everybody has a System 1, primed for action.

System 2 is a product of developmental education. Although Kahneman does not consider the educational implications of the 'bat and ball' problem they are profound. System 1 can be developed by teaching and learning designed to produce 'fast thinking'. For example we can all respond instantly to, *'What is two add two?'*, and even, *'What is two times two?'*, because familiarity and repetition have burned these responses onto our genetically inherited and incredibly efficient System 1. The educational theory of behaviourism (1.8) was based on the principle that all learning was about extending System 1 through repetition, punishment and reward. Most modern mainstream theories of learning including those underpinning the work described in this chapter are based on the developmental models of Piaget, Vygotsky and many others.

The following quotation from Vygotsky is so important it is worth repeating:

> As we know from investigations of concept formation, a concept is more than the sum of certain associative bonds formed by memory, more than a mere mental habit; it is a genuine and complex act of thought that cannot be taught by drilling, but can only be accomplished when the child's mental development has itself reached the requisite level.

Not only are such concepts a feature requiring Kahneman's System 2, but so also is the process of building the sophistication and power of the internalised individual concept structure that allows access to the higher Bloom levels of thinking. This, to a considerable extent, is what this book is about.

Marketisation of the education system has driven English classroom practice back towards System 1 behaviourism and away from the System 2 approaches that can make children more intelligent as they progress through a cognitively aware education system.

So what is the answer to the 'bat and ball' problem and why do even the best System 2 educated mathematicians and others often get it wrong? Kahneman states that even if you possess sufficient System 2 capability, you still get it wrong because *System 2 is lazy*. Firing up System 2 takes effort and if System 1 jumps to a convincing conclusion quickly enough, as it nearly always does, then System 2 is not even deployed even by the brightest and most expert.

Effective education is therefore not just about developing System 2 so it is able to cope with complex problems but also making us sufficiently mentally *resilient* that we routinely make the conscious effort of actually 'using our brains'. Johnston-Wilder and Lee's term, '*Developing Mathematical Resilience*' (5.4) is therefore well chosen and highly applicable to engaging our brain's System 2 capability.

Have you worked out the correct solution to the 'bat and ball' problem yet? No mathematical expertise is needed, just the resilience to *test* your System 1 answer.

If the ball costs 10p and the bat costs £1.00 more than the ball then the bat and the ball together must cost £1.20, not £1.10. Not difficult is it? So how do you get the answer? Try trial and error. The ball must cost less than 10p so try 5p. The bat now costs £1.05 giving a total of £1.10. So you have it: the ball costs 5p.

Before the GCSE C grade in maths became so grossly degraded every holder of this qualification, and many with lower grades, should have been able to apply the following simple algebraic solution to the problem rather than resort to trial and error.

Let the price of the ball be $x$ pence

Then the price of the bat must be $x + 100$

If the total price of bat and ball is 110 pence then:

$$x + (x + 100) = 110$$
$$2x + 100 = 110$$
$$2x = 10$$

Therefore $x = 5$

Slow thinking wins, and our education system needs much more of it.

## C 5.6 In praise of Sudoku

*My granddaughter, now nine years old, showed me a Sudoku puzzle and asked me what it was and how you solved it.*

*A Sudoku puzzle is a square 9 x 9 grid containing 81 squares. Within this there are 9 smaller 3 x 3 grids. Some of the squares are filled in with numbers from 1 to 9.*

*The task is to complete the grid by writing numbers in all the blank spaces such that every row, every column and every 3 x 3 box contains all the numbers from 1 – 9. There is only one solution to each puzzle.*

*Without my help it was clear that my granddaughter would not only have no idea where to start, she was also unable to understand what the task was, however she was excited about trying to solve it. Children that age love puzzles.*

*This was quite an easy Sudoku puzzle and we soon solved it together. She enjoyed this so I bought her a Sudoku puzzle book with 120 puzzles for £1.70 from Aldi. These were in a large format with one puzzle on each page that was not much smaller than A4. These puzzles were much harder.*

*I gave her a sharp pencil and an eraser and we sat down to look at the puzzle. I suggested to her that she could start with any row, column or 3 x 3 box and write in pencil (at the end of each row and column or in the corner of squares) what the missing numbers could be (i.e. the numbers from 1 to 9 not already in that row, column or 3 x 3 box). I further suggested that it might be best to start with the rows, columns or 3 x 3 boxes with least blank squares.*

*That is all the help I gave her. She soon got the idea and has become increasingly competent in solving the puzzles, which get harder as you progress through the book. She loves doing these and gets tremendous pleasure from the way the missing numbers rapidly fall into place as you get near the end of the puzzle.*

*Although I never described it as such, she soon understood the following general method for solving a Sudoku grid puzzle.*

*1. Start with a row, column or 3 x 3 box with the least numbers of blank squares.*

*2. Write in pencil all the possible missing numbers.*

*3. By inspecting the numbers already in the row, column or 3 x 3 box discount the numbers that do not fit (because they are already there).*

*4. If/when you get a unique solution for a blank square then write it in the grid.*

*5. When one row, column or 3 x 3 square has been fully completed tackle the next one with the least blank squares until the whole puzzle is completed.*

*I am a Sudoku novice. This method may not work for very hard puzzles.*

*My granddaughter is now very quick at solving the puzzles. Her working memory is now such that she can hold the possible numbers in her head. Not so her 67 year-old grandfather! She can now solve the puzzles faster than I can, but she still takes delight in us doing them together even though I just watch.*

*So what has been gained here? Not useful knowledge for sure. Who needs to know how to solve a Sudoku puzzle?*

*This is what has actually been understood by my granddaughter.*

*1. What an algorithm is – a sequential formula for solving a problem.*

*2. The logical operators NOT, AND and OR.*

*3. The programming instruction equivalent to IF ... THEN in BASIC*

*She is not aware that she understands these things in these terms (she does not know what an algorithm or a logical operator is), but I am certain that there has been significant cognitive development.*

*To me this has been confirmation of some of Vygotsky's fundamental tenets including the following.*

*1. The Zone of Proximal Development (ZPD) – what the child can do with the help of a more knowledgeable adult or peer, that cannot be achieved without such help and which facilitates cognitive development.*

*2. That the help provided should be minimal – just suggesting things to try.*

*3. That by such means children can understand and solve problems of surprising complexity.*

*4. That permanent cognitive development results, which is transferable to other subjects and contexts.*

*This is the sort of learning experience that children/pupils/students should meet and enjoy regularly (but of course not exclusively) in all Key Stages.*

*By these means students may progress in developing their cognitive sophistication levels and thus become generally cleverer.*

## 5.7 The Leicestershire Modular Framework

This is included as an example of teaching for cognitive development from a bygone era achieved at the level of the curriculum rather than individual lessons. Unless the reader is a teacher (or a pupil) of a certain age, what was happening in some Leicestershire schools in the late 1980s/early 90s may seem so esoteric and radical as to challenge the belief that it really happened at all. Yet it did, and I know because I was at the centre of it. Before the 1988 Education Reform Act the world of English schools was entirely different to the present day. I am not making a value judgment about this and will leave that to the reader – some will regard the period as thankfully discarded lefty anarchy. In those days individual teachers and schools had a very high degree of autonomy. There was no National Curriculum, no OfSTED, no government initiatives and no government involvement or interference whatever in the curriculum and teaching methods practised in schools.

This is not to paint a picture of an English education system of universal teacher driven radicalism. Most schools in the country remained staid institutions that had changed relatively little since the passing of the 1944 Education Act that established the principles of the post-war British education system. The character of local schools was strongly influenced, but not controlled, by Local Education Authorities (LEAs). This was exactly the intention of the 1944 Act. A uniform national framework of schools was created within which diversity on the basis of elected Local Authorities was encouraged, with freedom from government interference deliberately built into the system. This was in part a reaction to the then recent sinister history of state control of the school curriculum in Nazi Germany and the Soviet Union.

It took the election of Margaret Thatcher in 1979 to begin the dismantling of this consensus of non-interference in schools by the government. She is on record as stating that her greatest regret was not getting rid of 'left-wing' LEAs much sooner. However belated, Kenneth Baker's free market Education Reform Act eventually did the trick, with the new centralised powers further exploited by the 1997 Blair government. We now (2015) have an education system entirely managed and controlled by the government from London, with LEAs abolished in name and emasculated in function. Teachers have now largely become downgraded to educational operatives charged with 'delivering' the latest initiative, or at the whim of the personal prejudices of the sponsors/owners of the new Free Schools and Academies, be they powerful individuals, private companies and charities, or faith based religious organisations.

This sets the scene for the Leicestershire Modular Framework (LMF). The Leicestershire context is significant as this politically Conservative county was one of the first to enthusiastically go fully comprehensive based on 11-14 middle schools and 14-19 upper schools. Leicestershire upper schools became a stronghold for Mode 3 CSE courses (as distinct to the normal Mode 1 arrangement where the syllabus and the exams are set and marked by an external

Examinations Board). Mode 3 meant curriculum, assessment, exams (if any) and the awarding of grades all controlled and usually also designed by the pupils' own teachers. Mode 3 CSE courses could be either 'single school' or operated by voluntary consortia involving a number of schools joining forces.

In 1986, with the imminent replacement of CSE and GCE by the GCSE, there was a strong demand from Leicestershire's 14-18 upper schools to retain the principle of local control through the Mode 3 system. The new statutory criteria for the GCSE still provided for this and the Midland Examining Group, which became the local GCSE Board (before later privatisation), was open to local proposals as long as they met the new rules introduced by the government.

A group of Curriculum Deputies and Vice-Principals from Leicestershire schools (which by then for a while included the City of Leicester) formed a working group that produced the Leicestershire Modular Framework (LMF). This was first examined in 1988, with me as the Chief Examiner. LMF exploded in popularity and by 1991 most Leicestershire schools were entering pupils, together with a significant number outside the county as far away as Yorkshire.

It is easy to see with hindsight that such a scheme had no long term future in the culture that was being rapidly created by the 1988 Education Act. Teacher assessment and control of GCSE exams was obviously incompatible with a high stakes, league table driven system of market competition between schools and a culture of performance related pay based on exam results and league tables.

LMF was only ever intended for a minority of KS4 curriculum time in any given school. It was usually provided in GCSE option timetable blocks described as 'Additional Studies' taking up at most two subject's worth of time. A few schools, however, used LMF as the mainstream curriculum vehicle for core curriculum areas in Citizenship, Design and Technology, the Arts and the Humanities.

By 1991 there were 196 modules available to contribute to 10 possible subject titles. Many modules could count in more than one subject title. Five modules were needed for a GCSE qualification and all assessment was teacher based and could take a variety of forms. Standards were maintained by a process of moderation within and across centres, with ultimate approval for grading being certified by the GCSE Board. This was a normal, long established mainstream approach to 16+ examinations in Leicestershire, strongly supported by the LEA, which simply transferred its substantial Mode 3 administrative systems from CSE to the new GCSE. LMF enjoyed high level support from within County Hall.

The most radical feature of LMF was that assessment and accreditation were entirely content free (no stipulated knowledge content anywhere in the scheme) and based on a synthesis of Bloom and the Piagetian principles set out by Shayer and Adey in *Towards a Science of Science Teaching* (1981), which itself had strong Leicestershire roots. LMF was explicitly designed for the purpose of promoting and facilitating cognitive development, with any content knowledge gained along the way seen as a valuable bonus. Not all practitioners, however, saw it this way, with some using LMF primarily as a very effective approach for teaching their subject.

It was never the intention that the mainstream core curriculum in English, maths, science, humanities and a language (Gove's EBacc) should be taught on this scheme, however it *was* believed that the cognitive growth achieved by pupils who studied anything on the LMF framework would transfer to all their other studies. In one way the role of LMF at that time in Leicestershire schools could be seen as similar to that of the vocational studies (GNVQ, BTEC etc) that came much later, in that it usefully broadened the curriculum, but that is where any similarity ended. LMF was specifically designed to stretch and develop the intellect on the assumption that all pupils would be motivated through this process so long as cognitive demand was managed appropriately for individual pupils. Vygotsky's Zone of Proximal Development (ZPD) is relevant here. Maximum cognitive growth results when cognitive demand is just beyond that where the pupil can succeed comfortably without help. The teacher's job is to set up a curriculum framework and learning culture where the help is available in a variety of forms within a non-threatening, supportive social context that involves quality interactions with peers and the teacher.

GNVQ was primarily intended to boost GCSE results and the standing of schools in the league table. Any pupil motivation relied mainly on the dangled prize of multiple C grade passes guaranteed to all regardless of ability by following instructions and ensuring all the assessment boxes are ticked. This is behaviourism and it doesn't build cognitive growth.

LMF was assessed on the basis of a master grid of cognitive competences. The columns can be interpreted as ascending Piagetian and/or Bloom Levels. This assumed interchangeability between Piaget and Bloom is controversial. It can be argued that all the Bloom levels can be interpreted in all the Piagetian stages. It may be that Bloom has to be interpreted *in relation to* age or Key Stage. I am arguing that at KS4 Bloom's 'lower order thinking' is generally characterised by Piaget's 'concrete' stage, and 'higher order thinking' by Piaget's 'formal' stage. The LMF principle was certainly to promote cross curricular 'cognitive acceleration' gains like those claimed by Shayer and Adey.

The student was required to submit evidence for the purpose of assessment. This could take any form or combinations of forms that were fit for purpose including; a written folio (most common); a performance or series of performances; an artifact or group of artifacts or a written exam paper taken under exam conditions. The particular assessment requirements were written into each module, which had its own module specific Objectives and Attainment Grid that were used to award marks. All modules took the form of 'problems to be solved'.

Pupils were encouraged to work in groups, with the development of articulacy through peer-peer and student-teacher interactions at a small group level being encouraged.

| Assessment Objectives | Attainment Descriptors | | | |
|---|---|---|---|---|
| Cognitive Level | (1–2 marks) | (3–4 marks) | (5-6 marks) | (7-8 marks) |
| **A Recognition**<br><br>Recognise a problem or issue and plan a response | Can decide on a way to proceed | Can identify a number of alternative ways of proceeding | Can choose and develop an overall plan | Can develop an effective plan working through a range of alternatives and anticipating outcomes |
| **B Location**<br><br>Locate relevant information | Can find and identify appropriate information | Can select appropriate information, concepts, processes or skills | Can compare different concepts, processes and skills | Can gather and synthesise a range of concepts, processes and skills |
| **C Application**<br><br>Produce a solution or appropriate response | Can use simple information | Can apply appropriate information, concepts, processes or skills | Can apply in a co-ordinated way a range of concepts, processes and skills | Can synthesise a range of concepts, processes and skills with confidence and precision |
| **D Communication**<br><br>Produce an assessable outcome | Can produce a recognisable outcome | Can demonstrate purpose in the outcome | Can communicate the outcome of learning | Can communicate the structure, purpose and outcome of learning |
| **E Evaluation**<br><br>Evaluate conclusions and methodology | Can describe the task and the way it was done | Can describe the task and the way it was done and extract conclusions | Can identify the strengths and weaknesses of the methods used and draw conclusions from content | Can evaluate alternative methodologies applicable to the task |

*Figure 6 Master Objectives and Attainment Grid*

| Assessment Objectives | Module Attainment Descriptors | | | |
|---|---|---|---|---|
| Cognitive Level | (1–2 marks) | (3–4 marks) | (5-6 marks) | (7-8 marks) |
| A Recognition | Can decide on a way of how to find out how people lived during World War II | Can identify a number of ways of investigating people's experience of the war | Can choose and develop an overall plan for investigating people's experience of the war | Can develop a strategy that shows awareness of the strengths and weaknesses of alternative approaches |
| B Location | Can find some information about people's experience of World War II | Can find information from primary and secondary sources | Can make judgements about the quality of information obtained | Can synthesise, compare and evaluate evidence |
| C Application | Can use simple information to describe an aspect of people's experience | Can assemble an overall view of the challenges faced by people and their responses | Can relate people's experience to an understanding of key events during World War II | Can use the information obtained to make and justify historical statements about people's experience |
| D Communication | Can report on people's experiences and describe them in a folio | Can produce an organised folio setting out some reports of experiences from primary and secondary sources | Can communicate an overall view of people's experiences in an organised folio | Can produce a folio that relates people's experiences to historical events during World War II |
| E Evaluation | Can describe how the evidence was collected and how it was used | Can describe the task and the way it was done and draw some conclusions | Can comment on some strengths and weaknesses of the methods used and the conclusions drawn | Can compare alternative methodologies and the reliability of historical conclusions |

*Figure 7 Module Specific Example: Contemporary Accounts of World War II*

In the late 1980s most families had living witnesses to the war years. This module was about designing and implementing approaches to capturing those experiences. The method for combining module attainment was also radical. This was based on aggregating levels achieved on each objective A – E, but by aggregating marks across the programme, not within each module. Each level is identified by a cell in the grid, and then awarding the mark based on 'just' or 'well' satisfied. Hopefully higher levels would be achieved as pupils progressed through the scheme from the first to the fifth module so the final level for each objective for GCSE assessment could reasonably be the highest level achieved with the expectation that these would be found in the final modules. However real life does not always comply with expectations. Some method of aggregation that reflected the principle of cognitive development but having regard to anomalies like, four poor modules and one outstanding one, or performance getting worse on successive modules for diverse reasons, had to be addressed. This was achieved by the LMF 'Rule of Consistency' when aggregating attainment across modules.

The rule of consistency is that the highest mark is taken across the program provided that there are at least two other marks within one mark of it. If the highest mark does not meet the rule then the next highest is taken until the rule is satisfied. The following example shows how the system works.

| Module | Objective | | | | |
|--------|---|---|---|---|---|
| | A | B | C | D | E |
| 1 | 5 | 5 | 6 | 6 | 3 |
| 2 | 8 | 7 | 7 | 7 | 4 |
| 3 | 4 | 4 | 5 | 5 | 1 |
| 4 | 8 | 8 | 8 | 8 | 8 |
| 5 | 6 | 7 | 6 | 5 | 4 |
| Best Mark* | 7 | 8 | 7 | 7 | 5 |

Figure 8 Best mark using the 'rule of consistency'

This example achieved a total LMF programme score of 34 marks, which converts directly to a GCSE grade from the following table. In LMF all the assessment at GCSE grade level was in effect directly determined cell by cell across the grid, and since all the module grids were subsets of the master grid then GCSE standards were automatically maintained across all modules in the scheme. This example would produce a B grade GCSE (A* not yet invented).

| Total Programme Score | GCSE grade awarded |
|-----------------------|--------------------|
| 35-40 | A |
| 30-34 | B |
| 25-29 | C |
| 20-24 | D |
| 15-19 | E |
| 10-14 | F |
| 5-9 | G |
| 0-4 | U |

Figure 9 GCSE and Total Programme Score

I am not suggesting or proposing the reintroduction of LMF. I am however presenting this historic scheme as an example of how GCSE can be designed so as to assess and facilitate an approach to curriculum and learning based on cognitive development. Any teacher that has worked this way would be likely to apply the same kind of thinking to lesson planning even in traditional, formal, academic, linear courses. Provided of course the teacher was not under pressure to maximise C grades at all cost.

During 1988/89 I taught an LMF course to a group of Year 12 students at The Bosworth College, Leicestershire. It was timetabled for one afternoon per week as a form of General Studies type curriculum enrichment. I have retained some of the work from a module entitled, *Technology and Society*, which I interpreted so as to facilitate a study of two 'high rise' council housing developments. One was local, comprising the St Peter's estate in Leicester, and the other was the Park Hill estate in Sheffield. This latter was and remains highly innovative and controversial.

As well as the students researching both estates from available literature, the work included one half day visit to the St Peter's estate and a whole day trip to Sheffield. Both Leicester and Sheffield City Councils co-operated fully and arranged for the students to interview officers of the housing departments. Guided visits to the estates were provided, with the opportunity to interview residents. In Sheffield there were no difficulties, but the visit to the Leicester estate was more problematic and the Housing Department provided a highly respected local guide from the Residents' Association. There were ethnic tensions on the estate, so this was seen as a wise precaution. I would not have used this module with pupils in Years 10 or 11.

I include this recollection from my personal teaching as an example of how LMF could facilitate socially relevant, real life, cognitively demanding research for school students. Many of the students produced outstanding folios that I judge to be comparable to university undergraduate level work. I have no doubt that this module facilitated a significant degree of cognitive development in a very worthwhile learning context, perceived by the students to be both relevant and motivating.

## 5.8 Lessons from the nineteenth century

The Reverend Richard Dawes graduated from Cambridge, and became a mathematical tutor and bursar. He was something of a radical and upset his academic peers by advocating the admission of dissenters to the university. In 1837, he left Cambridge to become a country vicar in the parish of King's Somborne in Hampshire.

He adopted a novel approach to teaching based on engaging pupils through the examples of the 'common things' found in their everyday lives, which were used as objects of study and experimentation. In this he was anticipating Piaget and the later developmentalists in his emphasis on grounding lessons in practical activities to provide a 'concrete' foundation for progression to abstract theorising. Having his pupils enthusiastically undertake practical activities in groups indicates a social approach quite different from the normal punishment driven, authoritarian instruction and repetition typical of the period that is so powerfully described in the contemporary works of Charles Dickens.

Dawes' methods were extremely successful and gained the approval of leading national figures of the day in relation to the developing English education system.

James Bartholomew, describes him as follows in *The Welfare State We're In* (Politico 2004):

> Dawes took his pupils to the Roman road from Old Sarum to Winchester. He gave special attention to the way people lived at different periods — what sort of houses they had, what they ate and how they were clothed. He taught nature through the direct observation of local plants and trees, and through the study of birds and their migration. Under the supervision of the assistant master, the pupils kept records of barometric pressure and temperature. They kept a journal in which they recorded events such as the arrival of the first swallow, the coming of the cuckoo, the earliest pear and apple blossom and the first ears of wheat or barley. . .
>
> In mathematics the older boys learnt algebra and the subject matter of the first three books of Euclid. Again they used actual objects known to them — surveying the land around them and measuring in a carpenter's shop.
>
> Dawes proudly wrote: 'Writing in my study, I heard a noise of joyous voices, which I found proceeded from half-a-dozen boys, who after school hours, had come to measure my garden-roller.' They wanted to practise calculating the weight of a cylinder using measurements of the size and knowledge of the specific gravity of the material from which it was made.

It is clear that Dawes could not be criticised for any lack of ambition in what he expected his relatively poor rural children to comprehend.

In 1847 he published his masterpiece, which is a teacher's guide to how to implement his methods: *Suggestive Hints towards improved Secular Instruction*. Dawes insisted on cheap editions being widely available. Many editions were published. The 1857 7th edition can be viewed on-line:

http://archive.org/stream/suggestivehintsoodawegoog#page/n7/mode/2up

The scope of the book can be judged from the subtitle: Intended for the use of schoolmasters and teachers in our elementary schools, for those engaged in the private instruction at home, and others taking an interest in national education. This is an extract from the Introduction on p. 25:

> It is a fact almost unaccountable, and certainly curious to reflect upon, how few there are, even in any class of life, educated or uneducated, who are acquainted with the philosophical principles of those things which they see in action every day of their lives, and which are in so many ways administering to the wants of social life, - truths easily understood when explained by experiment, and so important in themselves to mankind, that the names of the discoverers of them are handed down from one generation to another for the admiration of future ages, and as the great benefactors of their species.

How very true, and how little has changed!

This book is remarkable, not just for its advanced approach to teaching and learning, but for its vast subject range, from English, through the humanities and the arts, to maths and science, demonstrating great scholarship and eclecticism in every subject area combined with a consistent pedagogic wisdom that pervades every chapter. As a retired teacher I continue to be inspired by it, and would dearly wish to repeat some of his lesson ideas. It should be compulsory reading for every trainee teacher today.

Dawes's village school made such a national impression that he was invited to write texts for teacher training. He was later appointed Dean of Hereford Cathedral. George Eliot described his face as "so intelligent and benignant that children might grow good by looking at it" (Oxford DNB).

Unfortunately however the enlightened example of Dawes did not herald a new wave of such progressive and effective teaching, and was snuffed out and largely forgotten following political changes later in the century. By the early 1860s, an economy-minded Liberal government wanted the state to get value for money. Grant payments were linked to pupils' success in basic tests in reading, writing and arithmetic. The system was dubbed 'payment by results'.

The following is taken from *Education in England: a brief history* by Derek Gillard (2011):

> A provision was introduced by the Committee of Council on Education into the Revised Code for 1862 (often called 'Lowe's Code' after the Committee's vice-president who devised it).

> The result of this regulation was the organisation of elementary schools on the basis of annual promotion. Classes in the senior

department were named standards I to VI, roughly corresponding to ages 7 to 12.

Right from the start there was much opposition to these arrangements. Teachers objected partly to the method of testing, but mainly to the principle of 'payment by results' because it linked money for schools with the criterion of a minimum standard. Thus the higher primary work which was beginning to appear before 1861 in the best elementary schools (My note: for example as in Dawe's school at Kings Somborne) was seriously discouraged by Lowe's Code. The curriculum became largely restricted to the three Rs, and the only form of practical instruction that survived was needlework.

Furthermore, the standards themselves were defective because they were based not on an experimental enquiry into what children of a given age actually knew, but on an a priori notion of what they ought to know. They largely ignored the wide range of individual capacity, and the detailed formulations for the several ages were not always precise or appropriate.

The philosophy of this dark period was shockingly close to the ideology of Michael Gove. How can recent government education policy be so ignorant not just of how children learn, but of the history of English education itself?

The darkest aspects of that history are being repeated 150 years later.

## C 5.8 More on the bucket theory of learning

The fate of the unfortunate Zarkov in Flash Gordon, (C1.8) will remind fans of Charles Dickens of the wretched pupils at the mercy of Thomas Gradgrind in Hard Times.

Although gloriously over the top, Thomas exemplifies the absurdity of the 'knowledge based' curriculum that is seeing a revival in some of our Academies and Free Schools. It is also worth comparing Gradgrind's pure form of 'bucket filling' as a theory of learning, with the richness of developmental practice in Richard Dawes' school in Kings Somborne.

The dates are interesting. Hard Times was first published in 1854. Dawes' masterpiece, Suggestive Hints towards improved Secular Instruction, was first published in 1847. The historical pedagogical tussle between the Dawes and Gradgrind approaches was resolved firmly in favour of Gradgrind.

By the early 1860s, an economy-minded Liberal government wanted the state to get value for money. Grant payments were linked to pupils' success in basic tests in reading, writing and arithmetic. The system was dubbed 'payment by results', and the methods of Gradgrind became the approved *method of educational delivery. Here are some quotes from Thomas Gradgrind and a visitor, presumably a school inspector, together confronting the pupils:*

*"Thomas Gradgrind now presented Thomas Gradgrind to the little pitchers before him who were to be so filled with facts...he seemed a kind of cannon loaded to the muzzle with facts, and prepared to blow them clean out of the regions of childhood at one discharge.*

*'Very Well', said this gentleman [the visitor], briskly smiling, and folding his arms. 'That's a horse. Now let me ask you girls and boys, would you paper a room with representations of horses?'*

*After a pause, one half of the children cried in chorus, 'Yes Sir! Upon which the other half seeing in the gentleman's face that Yes was wrong, cried out in chorus , 'No Sir!' – as the custom is in these examinations.*

*'I'll explain it to you, then', said the gentleman, after another and a dismal pause, 'why you wouldn't paper a room with representations of horses. Do you ever see horses walking up and down the sides of rooms in reality – in fact? Do you?'*

*'Yes sir!' from one half. 'No, sir!' from the other.*

*'Of course no,' said the gentleman, with an indignant look at the wrong half.*

*'Fact, fact, fact!' said the gentleman. And 'Fact, fact, fact!' repeated Thomas Gradgrind.*

*You are to be in all things regulated and governed,' said the gentleman, 'by fact. We hope to have , before long a board of fact, composed of commissioners of fact, who force the people to be a people of fact, and nothing but fact."*

## 5.9 Individual Personal Development, not a tyranny of Testing

In summary, the cognitive development of individual pupils should become the key objective of the primary and secondary school curriculum and there should be no place in our schools for cognitively depressing and intellectually suffocating practices like teaching to the test and press ganging pupils onto courses that make zero cognitive demands for the primary benefit of the school rather the student.

Teaching for cognitive development will *and should* result in pupil attainments covering the full range of grades from A*-G appropriately reflecting the bell curve distribution of cognitive ability in the general pupil population. Attaching school performance indicators to exam results that are not soundly related to the cognitive ability of individual pupils is counterproductive in educational terms and ultimately for all concerned in the education system.

School league tables based on crude performance indicators are an invitation to 'gaming' and a disincentive for schools to adopt the developmental approaches to learning that lead to cognitive growth. Mossbourne Community Academy (Part 4) is an exception made possible by the Hackney banded admissions system. Urban schools that can achieve balanced intakes have a degree of immunity from the worst perverse incentives. They can achieve without gaming (4.11, 4.14).

School league tables are also false indicators of school quality because their very nature precludes taking due account of the fact of continuously variable pupil cognitive ability.

The 1988 Education Act will eventually have to be repealed or drastically reformed. This current period of what I call 'Educational Lysenkoism' (after the ideological Soviet theory of agriculture that became the compulsory orthodoxy under Stalin) will eventually be consigned to history as an essential lesson in how not to run a national education system.

This is not going to happen easily or quickly but a start can be made. The first essential step is to challenge the fallacy of the denial of the role of cognitive ability in predicting and evaluating educational outcomes. The second is to promote the design of the curriculum for the cognitive growth of individual pupils, not the accumulation of high stakes, target-related qualifications for the school. The centrally controlled initiative roll-outs of New Labour rarely achieved the desired outcome and the free market based Academy and Free School project promoted by the Conservative led government is unlikely to be any more successful. So long as there are competitive school league tables driven by high stakes testing the education system will always be blighted and corrupted by perverse unintended outcomes arising from behaviourist incentives. Effective learning and national cognitive growth (a positive Flynn Effect) requires the liberation and encouragement of teachers and schools to investigate, discuss, devise and apply approaches designed to secure cognitive development at classroom and individual pupil level.

Local Education Authorities should be re-established, liberated, educated, empowered and encouraged to promote cognitively stimulating learning in all their schools. London Mayor Boris Johnson has stated he wants control of the London education system. He is right to recognise the need for locally administered schools. The Learning Trust in Hackney provides an example from which a start could be made.

The few remaining ex-LEA Education Department staff with knowledge and experience that have survived the era of 'Children's Services' reorganisation and the current cull of public sector employees should be attached to local school consortia to facilitate such shared work with more such experts trained and recruited. The disbanding of the Academies and Free School Division of the DfE would result in a multi £billion saving to the taxpayer that could be redirected for support of locally managed school improvement within a reformed culture.

University Schools of Education should again take a leading role informed by truly independent research. With competition between schools replaced by co-operation across schools (as has begun in Hackney) a start could also at last be made on restoring the sadly lost professionalism of teachers, which must be rooted in an appropriate degree of peer moderated classroom autonomy with regard to teaching methods, rather than 'operative' type 'delivery' of externally imposed initiatives. Only this, not performance related pay or 'fast tracking', will attract top graduates from the best universities back into a teaching profession with the necessary restored status.

## C 5.10 Lessons from America by Maurice Holt

Posted on LSN in August 2014

Maurice Holt is Emeritus Professor of Education, University of Colorado, Denver

*Ever since the Thatcher-Reagan love-in of the early 1980s, English education has taken its cue from developments in the US, united by a commitment to the Chicago school of neo-liberal economics which Reagan initially derided, only changing his tone when it became politic to do so. In England, the result of adopting Reagan-style outcome-led policies was Thatcher's flawed 1988 Education Act, which replaced local governance with central control and created Ofsted as a policing and enforcing device. Blair's 1997 administration might have moderated this approach, but instead it was embraced with enthusiasm.*

*One advantage, though, of the transatlantic-bridge tendency is that we can use American experience to prepare for what could happen here. With this in mind, I draw attention to a marvellous article which appeared recently (21 July 2014) in the New Yorker magazine, and which reveals the disturbing consequences of standardised testing once it dominates school process. Since access to the* New Yorker *is difficult without a subscription, a brief summary of this piece – "Wrong Answer," by Rachel Aviv – is offered below, followed by a few parallels with the current English context.*

*The driving force behind testing is the belief that assessing outcomes will tell you everything you need to know about teachers, students and school improvement. Neo-liberalism reinforces this, because markets function by comparing outcomes from competing providers: how they are reached is immaterial. The election of the Republican George W. Bush as president is key to this story, since his "No Child Left Behind" Act of 2002 depended on measurable outcomes as the key to school improvement. The basic idea was that by requiring a school's test results to improve year on year, students would learn more and American education would soon lead the world. After three or four years of this draconian legislation, its effects on schools were beginning to emerge: this is the point at which the* New Yorker *article begins. So we now turn our attention to the Parks Middle School, Atlanta, Georgia in spring 2006, where the consequences of outcome-based educational policy are influencing both teachers and students ...*

*The school is in a run-down area where half the homes are vacant and armed robberies are commonplace. Even so, the NCLB Act requires that all US students must take the Criterion-Referenced Competency Test, to implement federal achievement standards and also make "adequate yearly progress" by an annual increase in test scores. This legislation was based on a school accountability system used in Texas with – according to President Bush – amazing success. These claims have since been found wanting, but they helped to get Bush elected and they underpin his "No Child Left Behind" Act – which requires that all students in every school must achieve proficiency in maths and English as determined by test scores. Whether a student is lazy or lively, well-heeled or impoverished, is of no consequence: only the numbers have significance. If a school's progress falters, federal funding might be available. Conversely, without the stipulated improvement the school must be closed.*

*Parks Middle School had to reconcile the demands of the Act with the challenge of students living close to the poverty line: fewer than 40 per cent graduated from high school, and most came from broken homes. The schools superintendent for the district, however, had faith in the Bush remedy. She believed that public education could be improved by applying the values of the market place. She set school objectives for accountability and student performance, and if a school met its targets, every employee received a bonus. Teachers were evaluated on student test scores, and would be fired if their students failed to meet the targets within three years. The prevailing mantra was "No exceptions, no excuses." But how could the yearly improvement in test scores be met, with students from difficult backgrounds in a run-down area where crime was rife?*

*Inevitably, as teachers and principals came and went, it dawned on individual teachers that Parks students could not meet this classroom target, year on year. The students could not deliver enough right answers on the multiple-choice tests. If Parks was to stay in business, somehow the students' performance on the test papers had to be enhanced. Some teachers found a way to peek at the tests in advance, and then concentrate on teaching the examined topics. Or one could covertly gain access to the completed papers and change a few wrong answers to right ones, by erasing one blob and filling in another. Such conduct was professionally indefensible, but somehow the demands of the federal Act had to be reconciled with the impoverished homes of the students: then they might gain some encouragement and turn up for another year of schooling. Others might justify such extreme acts as a way of righting a wrong that stemmed from a misconceived view of education, and some gained reassurance when discovering, eventually, that other teachers were similarly engaged: as one remarked, "All our little problems that we grew up hiding from the rest of the world – it became our line of communication."*

*There were four sub-superintendents in the school district, who subjected teachers to mid-term reviews. In the case of Parks Middle School, one teacher's review read, "Please understand that no excuse can or will be accepted for any results that are less than 70 per cent of school-based target acquisition." The teacher replied that the targets were unrealistic, that it took three months just to gain a student's trust, and some students lived alone with neither parent at home. Indeed, the need to enhance student scores was recognised unofficially by the principal, since if the school didn't reach its annual target it would be liquidated and the students moved to schools further away – which would be a discouragement to learning.*

*Matters came to a head when a sixth-grade teacher complained to the district superintendent that the principal was attempting to persuade teachers to cheat, and the local teachers' federation complained to the district central office that the principal was intimidating staff. A private investigator was hired, and concluded that some teachers had cheated on the Georgia Middle Grades Writing Assessment. But no action was taken, and the following year the school had to score even higher than before, in accordance with federal law. One teacher remarked that the legislators who wrote the No Child Left Behind Act must never have been near a school like Parks. But the legislation was entirely in accordance with the strictures laid down by President Reagan back in the 1980s, who argued that the entire US school system was in crisis because of lazy teachers and lack of accountability. (One could argue that a similar attitude, on the part of Mrs*

*Thatcher, led to her flawed 1988 Education Act.) Reagan's view was challenged at the time by David Berliner, then professor of education at Arizona State University, who suggested in his persuasive book The Manufactured Crisis (1995) that these criticisms were unfounded: there was no crisis until Reagan invented one. Berliner has since been in touch with Rachel Aviv (author of the* New Yorker *article) and pointed out that the "No Child Left Behind" legislation in effect asked teachers to compensate for factors outside their control: "The people who say poverty is no excuse for low performance are now using teacher accountability as an excuse for doing nothing about poverty." This is, of course, the position taken by recent English education ministers: it is all the fault of lazy teachers, to which payment by results is the only solution.*

*Since Parks Middle School had to show test-score improvement or die, at each year's end the secretive massaging of test scores continued: no one discussed it, but teachers had gained access to the room of the school's testing coordinator, and the principal made no secret of the need to enhance those scores. And so, by 2009, it emerged that 90 percent of eighth graders had passed the exam: Parks was hailed as an outstanding school, winning a "Dispelling the Myth" award (sic) and gaining national prominence. But a month later, two reporters on the Atlanta* Journal-Constitution *discovered that the testing gains at Parks, and at some other Atlanta schools, were statistically unlikely. The governor asked the state attorney general to investigate after the discovery that one in five Georgia schools showed erasure marks on the test papers.*

*It has since emerged that cheating took place in forty other states; Atlanta was one of the few that subpoenaed educators, after finding that 44 schools had cheated and that "a culture of fear, intimidation and retaliation has infested the district." Nine teachers and officials were sacked, and the scores of Parks students then dropped each year. Now, however, the stakes for testing in Georgia have been raised: a new teacher-evaluation program bases 50% of the assessment on test scores, and is combined with a merit-pay system. The authority has learned nothing and forgotten nothing.*

*This summary of the* New Yorker *article does scant justice to a valuable account of a misguided way to improve education. But it will strike a familiar chord with teachers in England, since the current government is totally in thrall to the doctrine that the quality of education can be determined by assessing outcomes. When I took up my post in Denver in 1991, I soon heard about a pundit who had declared that the future lay with outcome-based education. One or two local school districts had responded, and begun the task of deciding which outcomes would need to be measured. But then came the problem of determining how a desirable quality like "the ability to work cooperatively" could be numerically assessed in a reliable* fashion. *Fortunately, Denver has a high proportion of thoughtful graduates, and the weakness of this approach soon became evident. But recent English ministers of education are obsessed by outcomes, forever revising examinations and syllabuses and burdening teachers with demands for data. They have yet to recognise the importance of process, and of approaches like the slow-education movement which address process.*

*As W.E.Deming has remarked, to try to improve process by studying outcomes "is like driving by looking in the rear-view mirror." Meanwhile, teacher morale in English schools continues to decline, and devices like recruiting new graduates directly into teaching – another American idea – are merely an expedient. The full implications of this focus on measurable outcomes have yet to emerge, and perhaps a change of government in 2015 will herald a more intelligent approach to school improvement. In the meantime, America's love affair with testing dogma continues: President Obama's "Race to the Top" program for raising test scores is simply a variant of George W Bush's legislation – now generally referred to in the US as the "No School Left Undamaged" Act. Schools in England must contend with the increasing influence of Ofsted (now costing more than £200m annually), with its increasing prominence as an arm of government, and with the looming impact on teachers of performance-related pay – an infallible strategy for undermining trust and creating ill will. At least the staff at Parks Middle School were united against a common enemy: to destroy team spirit by setting teachers in competition with each other is a recipe for disaster.*

## 5.10 School improvement and the Anti-Flynn effect

The start of my personal journey that has led to this book was our *TES* investigation (3.1) into claimed school improvement (Titcombe & Davies 2006). We took the 2004 '100 most improved schools' list published by the then named Department for Education and Skills (DfES) and attempted to analyse the 2005 GCSE and equivalent results of all the schools on a subject by subject, grade by grade basis. A further control group of 60 'unimproved' schools was also investigated in the same way. We found a direct relationship between the degree of school improvement and decreased opportunity for pupils to take high cognitive demand academic subjects. In some schools there was no opportunity to take GCSE science (rather than a 'vocational equivalent') at all. The curriculum areas that were being degraded in the most improved schools were the very ones later identified by Michael Gove as being so important as to require a special place in league tables. These then constituted the English Baccalaureate (Ebacc). It was the 'unimproved', 'coasting' schools that were actually providing the best and most enabling curriculum opportunities for their pupils.

In Part 3 this issue was revisited showing that little had changed over the intervening period from our 2005 research. The 2010 'most improved' schools, with 30+ percentage points improvement since 2007, achieved on average only 5.6 percent of pupils meeting the Ebacc standard compared with 15.6 percent for all schools (3.8). Intervening levels of improvement were negatively correlated with Ebacc performance.

If the 'most improved' schools are providing the worst educational opportunities and the government reacts by forcing schools to 'improve further and faster' on the same ideological model then the cure is clearly killing the patient. In Part 3 I also predicted further perverse outcomes from attempts to remedy curriculum distortions by further fiddling with the league tables. Some of these are already emerging such as beginning KS4 in Year 8 or 9 and systematic early GCSE entry to maximise C grade passes in cognitively demanding subjects.

Shayer and Ginsburg (2009) found a large decline in average cognitive performance of English 14 year-old pupils over the preceding 30 years and called this the 'Anti-Flynn' effect (see 1.4).

## 5.11 Children have become less able than they used to be

Two major studies carried out by Michael Shayer and his co-workers, Shayer M , Ginsburg D & Coe R (2007) and Shayer M & Ginsburg D (2009),  suggest that between the 1970s and the early years of the current century the Flynn Effect (1.4) has gone into reverse in English schools. James Flynn found a pattern in all countries with national state funded education systems of average IQ scores tending to increase year on year such that standardised tests like Cognitive Ability Tests (CATs) have to be re-standardised about every fifteen years.

The first piece of research was with Y7 pupils and produced startling evidence of a developmental decline. The second study on Y9 pupils produced evidence of an even greater decline. This was so unexpected and dramatic that the first study became the subject a *Guardian* article of 24 January 2006 by John Crace, even before the work was peer reviewed and published:

> It has become an annual rite of summer. Out come the Sats/GCSE/A -level results - take your pick - and up pops a government minister to say that grades are higher than ever, teachers and schools have done a fantastic job, but there's still room for improvement. Not everyone takes this at face value and

there are a few grumbles about exams becoming easier. But even if there are suspicions that standards have dropped, no one has ever seriously suggested that children's cognitive abilities have deteriorated. Until now. New research funded by the Economic and Social Research Council (ESRC) and conducted by Michael Shayer, professor of applied psychology at King's College, University of London, concludes that 11- and 12-year-old children in year 7 are "now on average between two and three years behind where they were 15 years ago", in terms of cognitive and conceptual development.

## Michael Shayer was quoted as follows:

It's a staggering result. Before the project started, I rather expected to find that children had improved developmentally. This would have been in line with the Flynn effect on intelligence tests, which shows that children's IQ levels improve at such a steady rate that the norm of 100 has to be recalibrated every 15 years or so. But the figures just don't lie. We had a sample of over 10,000 children and the results have been checked, rechecked and peer reviewed.

Shayer's wife, scientist Denise Ginsburg, was regularly employed by schools to run their Year 7 maths and science developmental testing to see which children needed Shayer and Adey's Cognitive Acceleration programmes (5.2).

She reported that she had begun to notice a significant falling off in children's abilities. Because of this Shayer decided to investigate further. His first research project involved the assessment of 10,000 year 7 children's performance on developmental volume and heaviness tests.

The second project found a similar negative effect on the attainment of 'Formal Operations (1.7, 5.2) by Y8 and Y9 compared with 1976. Shayer put the cause down to: "either a change in general societal pressures on the individual, or in the style of teaching in schools, or both."

If Shayer is right, then the question that must be answered is why children's developmental skills have fallen off so much. Shayer has speculated about the possible lack of experiential play in primary schools, and the growth of a video-game, TV culture. Both take away the kind of hands-on play that allows children to experience how the world works in practice and to make informed judgments about abstract concepts.

I think he could be right about this but he is ignoring the significant effect of the national Nuffield Science Initiative in the 1970s that substantially changed the science curriculum in favour of large scale experimentation and hypothesising by pupils. Looking back from my own experience as a science teacher at that time, this process was very positive in Piagetian developmental terms.

Plenty of other explanations have been offered from a variety of sources. As usual the political left favours social and environmental explanations like poor nutrition and computer games. The right tends to resort to dubious genetic arguments involving differential procreation rates and immigration.

I am accepting Shayer's conclusions of real cognitive decline and proposing a wholly educational explanation for what are educational phenomena.

My hypothesis, an invitation for others to argue about, is that degraded and corrupted curriculum involving the large scale abandonment of pupil practical activity in science lessons and the increased substitution of crude behaviourism for developmentalism as the ruling pedagogy in English schools, combined with successive perverse outcomes arising from the operation of the imposed market are combining to produce an ever tightening spiral of real educational decline that continues to manifest itself in new and often surprising ways.

## 5.12 Performance Related Pay: the Problem, not the Solution

The favourite remedy of the political right for the alleged failings of our teachers, and consequently our schools, is performance related pay (PRP). The argument goes that as teachers vary in their ability to get their pupils to pass exams so they should be paid by the exam results of their classes. Only by dangling financial incentives can people be motivated to work hard.

One of many fundamental problems with such an approach is that pupils vary enormously in their ability to comprehend and make progress, not to mention all the personal emotional baggage that children bring to their lessons.

Consider a secondary school that might have six full time maths teachers whose work is organised and managed by a Head of Department, who is also a very able and experienced classroom teacher. Her department would be likely to comprise teachers of varying age, experience and competence. The KS4 classes would most likely be setted according to ability. Each year the Head of Department would have the job of allocating classes to her teachers (and to herself). On the principle that all pupils, regardless of ability, have the right to be taught by the best teachers it would not be right for there to be a hierarchy of teachers with regard to who gets the 'best' (easiest to teach) and 'worst' (hardest to teach) classes. It is clearly best for all pupils if classes are shared out from year to year. This is also best for teachers because even if all other personal attributes are equivalent, teachers become more competent with experience. Such experience can only be gained by being exposed to the huge variety of demands presented by children of vastly different abilities and social backgrounds. Such arrangements are the only way that an effective Head of Department can develop her team over a period of years. Of course teachers have individual talents and enthusiasms and a wise Head of Department would also want to take these into account.

So how would payment by results work? Much of this book has been about the fact that pupils of lower cognitive ability on average can reasonably and rightly be expected to get lower exam grades. They are also likely to make slower progress. Differential payments to teachers (decided by whom on what basis?) would result in the destruction of all sense of common purpose, teamwork and professional co-operation within the department. Far from passing on advice to less experienced colleagues, the opposite would result. One teacher's personal access to a limited bonus pool would depend on the *relative* performance of all the teachers in the school so each individual teacher's strategy for maximising her pay would involve not just her classes getting better results but her colleagues classes getting worse. We have seen in Part 3 what can happen to standards in a high stakes results based culture. It is hard to imagine a more destructively perverse incentive in a school. This is pure behaviourism, and regrettably it is already degrading standards in our schools as Academies are bringing the management practices of business and the 'bonus culture' into the education system. The bonuses always seem to be greater the further you rise in the hierarchy and the less teaching you do. Free Schools will have even more such 'freedoms'.

Then there is the question of the pastoral system of the school. How would payment by results be applied to Heads of Year and Form Tutors? Would a form teacher's pay be affected by the number of persistent truants in her form, and how would pastoral staff be rewarded for their contribution to the academic success of pupils whose personal problems they had successfully addressed? Most destructive of all would be the gradual realisation by all the teachers in the PRP system, that it was individual less bright, more badly behaved and poorly attended pupils that stood between them and their performance bonuses. This would not promote a healthy staff/pupil relationship culture.

There is however a sense in which payment by results is perfectly reasonable and has existed in schools for decades. There are (were) differentiated pay scales and allowances for responsibilities. Unfortunately the changes made to teachers' pay and conditions in recent years have tended to erode and constrain, rather than extend such differentiation, which recognises and rewards experience, expertise and responsibilities.

The best way to hold teachers to account and deal with underperformance is to be fully open and transparent about the pay and job description of every single employee in the organisation. This means publishing the pay, pay scale and detailed job description and schedule of responsibilities for every teacher including the Senior Management Team and the headteacher or 'Executive Principal' as she is now more likely to be called. This information should be publicly available to anybody and everybody, obviously including governors and parents. This was the system in my headship school and it caused no problems at all. When you are paid from the public purse the public has a right to know exactly how much you are paid and what you are expected to do for it.

Such a system would be met with shock and horror in the English world of business, but it is completely normal in more successful economies, especially in Scandinavia where anyone can look at anybody else's pay and tax returns with a few clicks of a mouse on a personal computer. If the business world doesn't like it they don't have to do it, but neither should inferior systems be imposed on schools by people that don't know any better.

The transparency approach also provides a sound structure for accountability. All teachers have line managers with specified responsibilities for the performance, individually and collectively, of their teams. There should be no 'performance bonuses' of any kind – ever. Everybody is expected to do the job they are paid for. It really is as simple as that. Some individuals will outgrow their current job and wish to apply for a more highly paid one, either within the same school or elsewhere. Some individuals may be failing to meet the requirements of their job description, so line managers have to address that through established procedures and fair processes. Obviously nobody should be sustained in a job they are not doing properly or retained in such a job if, after receiving appropriate support, they still can't do it effectively.

I had a number of jobs in the private sector before I became a teacher and saw plenty of petty status seeking, fiddling, skiving, idling and much worse besides. In contrast when I first became a teacher in 1971 I was surprised by what was expected of me in terms of hours, expertise and professionalism and I was in awe of the very high standards of many of my more experienced colleagues, who taught me everything I know about schools.

## C 5.12 When effort becomes exhaustion by Melissa Benn

*Posted on LSN in April 2014.*

*"Do you know a ghost child? Are you possibly raising one?" A report this week by the Association of Teachers and Lecturers (ATL) pinpoints a worrying new phenomenon – the institutionalised infant, a whey-faced creature, stuck in school for 10 hours a day, the child of commuting parents possibly, wandering from playground to desk to after-school club without real purpose, nodding off through boredom and fatigue.*

*The sad thing is, as yet another timely ATL report brings home, the ghost child is increasingly likely to be taught by the ghost adult – a teacher grey with fatigue and stress, stuck at school for 10 hours or more a day, wandering from duty to duty in playground, classroom or after-school club. Both, it seems, are part of a culture that increasingly overworks our citizens, from a younger and younger age, in the often fruitless quest for job security and social mobility.*

*We know the figures. England is one of the most overworked European nations. What's really new is that we no longer question or even quarrel with this fact. Instead we deploy American-lite righteousness. Work is now not merely a sign of virtue, it is a sign of proper panic, of appropriately anxious aspiration. Any other approach takes you right down benefits street.*

*Such values have easily transferred to education, where decades of inequality in provision and under-investment have neatly reduced the problems in our system to one of effort, or the lack of it. When a few years ago I interviewed Sir Michael Wilshaw, then still head of Mossbourne academy, he brimmed with anger at "clockwatching" teachers whom he believed had failed to bring poorer pupils on.*

*Concerns like these have now morphed into a settled theory of education, and childhood itself. Educational reform now largely equals intensive schooling: early-morning catch-up classes, after-school clubs, longer terms, shorter holidays, more testing, more homework.*

*The trouble is, the human body and human communities do not flourish through being flogged. Families don't benefit from frenetic rushing. They simply forget who each other is, or could be, which is where the real problems begin. Overtired children don't learn. And hungry overtired children simply fall asleep, or kick off.*

*We could have learned this years ago from some of the most impressive education systems in the world, where children do not start formal learning till as late as seven – and certainly not at two, the scary suggestion now being made by some in government – and where the school day is much shorter. Visitors to some of the Nordic countries, including Finland – still the highest-performing system in Europe – report that it can look as if the children are doing very little in the classroom. There, the educational conversation is all about deep flourishing, enjoyment, stimulation of a different kind.*

*That makes sense, right? Some of the most productive, and highly professional, people I know work relatively short days and even seem to spend an awful lot of time in contemplation: reading, thinking, staring into space. As one eminent academic said to me, puzzled at so much manic activity in modern living: "I have never worked a 15-hour day in my life."*

*And the language of effort will not eradicate – only possibly obscure – the educational inequalities that have shifted remarkably little over my lifetime. A poor child on site gets a much-needed breakfast and long hours of subsidised childcare. A better-off child is more likely to be wheeled around to all sorts of extracurricular activities that might make them fractious and overtired but will surely enrich them, in every way, later in life.*

*This government won't shift gears. It is fully signed up to the ghost road, particularly for the poor. But in other more interesting spaces and places there is a return to ideas that celebrate a different approach to learning, earning and being a human being.*

*The New Economics Foundation recently proposed that we should make "part time ... the new full time" – that by sharing employment in a time of austerity, with some guarantee on income, of course, we create more time for everyone, old and young alike, to do the things that make us human: spend time with family, friends, take a walk, read a book.*

*John White, the brilliant philosopher of education, has long argued that "schools [should] be mainly about equipping people to lead a fulfilling life". Anthony Seldon, the master of Wellington College, home of the much-celebrated "happiness lessons", would surely agree. And the wonderful movement for "slow education" stresses the importance of process over pushing, quality over endless quantifying. "The notion of slow ... fosters intensity and understanding and equips students to reason for themselves ... the arts of deliberation are an essential element in this." according to its architect Maurice Holt.*

*Of course, such notions are utterly unGoveian. Fiendishly Finnish in fact. At their heart is the radical idea that time itself – time to think, time to laugh, time to potter, time at home, time alone – should make a comeback in pedagogical and human discourse. Our growing army of ghost children deserve nothing less."*

This was my response on LSN:

*"Melissa – Your post is so timely and correct. Every time I hear a Tory minister or MP spout about 'hard working families' I am consumed with anger and frustration. This is the root cause of the scandal of exhausted children that you so rightly highlight.*

*I recently rediscovered the Apprenticeship Indenture of my father, dated 13 January 1936 on his leaving secondary school. It reads: 'John Ackworthie Ltd (of Birmingham) agree to instruct him in the art of Toolfitting, which he now useth in the manufacture of Engineer's Tools and will also pay the following scale of wages (weekly): 1st year 10/- (50p) 2nd ; 12/6 3rd ; 15/- 4th ; 20/- 5th ; 25/- 6th ; 30/- 7th ; 35/- (£1.75) An ordinary working week to count of 47 hours. Overtime to be paid at double the ordinary rate.'*

*From that date my father was in continuous well paid employment in Engineering work in Birmingham until after Thatcher was elected in 1979.*

*1936 was the height of the Great Depression, yet my dad left school with no exam passes and gained an apprenticeship that provided guaranteed employment and training for seven years, a very large guaranteed annual percentage pay rise every year for seven years and a contractual 47 hour week (no unsocial hours) with double hourly pay for overtime. I don't know what his pay rates are equivalent to now, but my guess is that they are better than the minimum wage for 16 year old school leavers and he was younger than that. Present day school leavers eat your heart out. I was born in 1947 and brought up on a low rent Birmingham council estate. There was never, ever any sense that we lived in 'social housing'. We had a TV, a fridge, a twin tub washing machine and a vacuum cleaner, but no car and one week per year family holiday by the seaside. It was a happy childhood. We were never cold or hungry or badly clothed. My mother only worked after I started secondary school in 1958. My father's working week was about 45 hours, but overtime was always paid. He was a lifelong member of the Amalgamated Engineering Union. Of course we should be angry about the direction of travel under the Conservatives-led coalition..*

*But what about Labour? Can we really accept such limited ambition that does not even amount to a promise of better and healthier lifestyles than in 1936?"*

Henry Stewart responded as follows:

*"Intriguing information, Roger. Average salary in 1936 appears to have been £150 a year, compared to £25,000 now. Minimum apprenticeship*

*rates are £5,000 (20% of the average), so your dad's rate quickly rose above that and was 50% of the average salary by the end of the period."*

*Surely we can provide better opportunities for our school leavers than my father experienced in the Great Depression of 1936?*

*For the sake of our children and grandchildren we have to demand this.*

## 5.13 Time for a new paradigm?

As a scientist I recognise the work of Thomas Kuhn in producing a theory of competing paradigms to explain the history of dominant scientific theories. Trevor Fisher (2011) has made a useful contribution by analysing the post-war English education system in terms of such Kuhnian paradigms.

He argues that in the field of education these can also be seen as intellectual structures that determine what evidence is accepted and what is rejected with outcomes that are often irrational. He accepts the CFBT report of 2010, *Instinct or Reason: How Education Policy is made* in seeing government education policy imperatives as not being primarily driven by evidence.

Fisher identifies three historical paradigms in the post-war English education system.

1: The tripartite paradigm

This was embedded in the 1944 Education Act and divided secondary schools into three types; grammar, technical and secondary modern, with entry determined by the 11-plus IQ test, which categorised children into distinct groups for life. Technical schools soon disappeared leaving only grammars and secondary moderns.

2: The comprehensive paradigm

This creation of the Harold Wilson Labour government followed, and persisted up to the 1988 Education Act, which was a deeply ideological framework designed to establish the foundation for a market driven education system. Margaret Thatcher has stated that her greatest regret in government was to have waited so long since the 1979 General Election brought her to power, before moving to destroy what she regarded as left wing education authorities and the influence of left wing educationalists.

3: The marketisation paradigm

This was enshrined in the 1988 Act and further developed by the Blair and Brown Labour governments by the fragmentation of the education system through the introduction of numerous categories of schools including Grant Maintained, Specialist and culminating in commercially sponsored, but taxpayer funded independent schools, which it called Academies. The Conservative led coalition government of 2010 has attempted to extend the Academy model to all schools and introduced a new category of taxpayer funded, even more independent schools, called Free Schools, that can in theory be set up by anybody that the Secretary of State approves of.

The thrust of Kuhn is that paradigms acquire a high degree of inertia and are not easily abandoned. Contradictory evidence is not enough until the amount and quality of such evidence reaches a tipping point. Where the paradigm has been adopted by the state as an official orthodoxy it is especially hard to overcome. The Lysenko agricultural paradigm in the Soviet Union required mass starvation on an apocalyptic scale before it was finally superseded in an agricultural Kuhnian revolution. The Secretary of State for Education at the time of writing this book, Michael Gove, up to his sacking in July 2014, appeared to be showing a similar neo-Stalinist attitude to the school system in his desire to control what children must learn and how they must be taught in our schools. It will therefore require a Kuhnian educational revolution to supersede this decline that is engulfing our schools.

My hope is that this book will provide a significant further nudge towards the necessary tipping point that can eventually save, reform and revive the English education system.

## C 5.13 A step by step way forward

Evolution is better than imposed revolution. Step by step structural change is possible in the English education system. Here are my suggestions for the stages. It is very important that each relatively small step itself represents a significant improvement on what went before. This replaces ideology with pragmatism and promotes a culture of apolitical professional ownership of the system.

1. Reform Ofsted by replacing it with an independent, directly employed HMI answerable directly to parliament (as Ofsted once falsely claimed it was).

2. Reform local government by recreating LEAs and Education Committees. A by-product would be the abolition of 'Cabinet' government so re-democratising and reinvigorating Local Government. At the same time, promote the creation of unitary LAs where possible especially in urban areas.

3. Give the new LEAs regulatory power and responsibility over the admissions policies of all the schools in their area, including Academies and Free Schools, so as to promote balanced, all ability intakes. Something quite close to this has already come about in Hackney through voluntary

*agreements. The Hackney model is a good one. It is especially appropriate for urban areas.*

*4. Produce a national funding formula for all schools, Academies, Free Schools and LEA schools alike.*

*5. Reform the powers and constitution of the governing bodies of all schools including Academies and Free schools with places reserved for elected teachers parents and local councillors, with safeguards created to stop organised groups gaining power through infiltration to promote narrow sectarian or religious objectives.*

*6. Require all schools to produce an annual prospectus to a specified template that includes the curriculum, behaviour and other policies, including full exam results in the subject by subject, number of passes at each grade format, that used to be required. Cease the publication of aggregated attainments (eg %5+A\*-Cs or anything that may replace it) and so abolish school league tables. Abolish all general floor targets for schools.*

*7. Abolish KS2 SATs to be replaced by CATs taken in Y6 alongside other specific diagnostic, standardised assessments. DfE to continue to publish on the internet sound and valid technical data that it expects LEAs to use for the local inspections of all schools in its area.*

*8. HMI to conduct periodic inspections of all schools alongside LEA inspectors. LEA inspectors to provide CPD and school support for all schools (including Academies and Free Schools) with the help of HMI when requested.*

*9. HMI to inspect LEAs and Academy/Free School chains, all on the same basis.*

*10. Require parents' referenda on the governance and control of Academy and Free schools if a threshold proportion of parents sign a petition according to a standard template. This would give local communities the democratic power to restore failing Academies to LEA control.*

*11. Create a permanent National Educational Commission with a carefully designed constitution with academic, professional and political appointments on a non-party basis to advise all forthcoming governments on education policy, and so take our schools out of politics.*

*Courage and inspiration is now needed to repair the damage and to create a new model of social ownership, control and accountability of public services. This especially applies to education.*

# Bibliography

Adey, P., Shayer, M. (1981) *Towards a Science of Science Teaching.* London: Heinemann Educational Books.

Adey, P., Shayer, M. (1994) *Really Raising Standards: Cognitive Interventions and Academic Achievement.* London: Routledge.

Adey, P., Shayer, M. (2002) *Learning Intelligence.* Open University Press.

Adey, P., Dillon J. (2012) *Bad Education.* Open University Press.

Bartholomew, J. (2001) *The Welfare State We're In.* London: Politico.

Bloom, B. S., Engelhart, M.D., Furst, E.J., Hill W.H., & Krathwohl D. R. (1956) *Taxonomy of educational objectives: the classification of educational goals; Handbook I: Cognitive Domain.* New York: Longmans.

Cheney, C.D., & Ferster, C.B. (1997) *Schedules of Reinforcement (BF Skinner Reprint Series).* Copley Publishing Group.

Claxton, G., (2006). *Expanding the capacity to learn.* BERA Annual Conference: University of Warwick.

Dawes, R., (1857) *Suggestive Hints towards improved Secular Instruction.* Groombridge and Sons.
[Online]
Available at:
http://archive.org/stream/suggestivehints00dawegoog#page/n7/mode/2up

De Waal, A., (2009) *The Secret of Academy's Success.* Civitas Report. [Online]
Available at:
www.civitas.org.uk/pdf/secrets_success_academies.pdf

Demos, (2011) *The Forgotten Half.*
[Online]
Available at: www.demos.co.uk/publications/theforgottenhalf

Fisher, T., (2011) *Considering the big picture: how significant are policy initiatives?* Educational Review, 63(4).

Flynn, J., (2009) *What Is Intelligence: Beyond the Flynn Effect.* Cambridge: Cambridge University Press.

Flynn, J. R., (1987) *Massive IQ gains in 14 nations: What IQ tests really measure.* Psychological Bulletin, Issue 101, pp. 171-191.

Gardner, H., (1983) *Frames of Mind: The Theory of Multiple Intelligences.* New York: Basic Books.

Gillard, D., (2011) *Education in England: A brief history.*

[Online] available at: www.educationengland.org.uk/history

Gould, S., (1981) *The Mismeasure of Man*. New York: WW Norton.

Hutton, W., (2011) *Them and Us: Changing Britain – Why we need a Fair Society*. London: Abacus ed.

Inhelder, B., Piaget J., (1958) *The Growth of Logical Thinking from Childhood to Adolescence*. Routledge & Kegan Paul.

IPSO MORI, (2013)
[Online]
Available at: http://www.ipsos-mori.com/Assets/Docs/Polls/Feb2013_Trust_Topline.PDF
[Accessed 22nd March 2014].

Jefferson, T., (1787) *Constitution of the United States*.
[Online]
Available at: http://www.wdl.org/en/item/2708/
[Accessed 10th September 2014].

Johnston-Wilder, S. Lee, C., (2010) *Developing mathematical resilience*. University of Warwick.

Kahneman, D., (2011) *Thinking, Fast and Slow*. New York: Penguin.

Shayer, M. D., Ginsberg, R., & Coe, R.D., (2007) *Thirty years on -- a large anti-Flynn effect? The Piagetian test Volume and Heaviness norms*. British Journal of Educational Psychology, 77(25-41).

Shayer, M.,Ginsberg, D., (2009) *Thirty year on -- a large anti-Flynn effect/(II) 13 and 14-year-olds. Piagetian tests of formal operations norms 1976-2006/7*. British Journal of Educational Psychology, Volume 79, pp. 409-418.

Mansell, W., (2008) *Education by Numbers – The Tyranny of Testing*. London: Politico.

Mortimer, P., Scott P., (2003) *Meaning Making in Secondary Science Classrooms*. Open University Press.

Mortimore, P., (2011) *Markets are for Commodities, Not Children*. Forum, 53(3).

Petty, G., (2014) *Evidence-Based Teaching*. 2nd ed. Oxford: Oxford University Press.

Pinker, S., (2002) *The Blank Slate*. London: Penguin.

Herrnstein R.J., Murray, C., (1994) *The Bell Curve*. 1st ed. New York: Simon and Schuster.

Randall V., Bass, R.V., & Good, J.W., (2004) *The Education Forum*. Volume 68.
[Online]
Available at: http://files.eric.ed.gov/fulltext/EJ724880.pdf
[Accessed 22nd March March 2014].

Russell Group, (2011) *Informed Choices.*
[Online]
Available at: www.russellgroup.ac.uk/informed-choices

Saunders, P., (2010) *Social Mobility Myths.* London, Civitas.

Saunders, P,. (2012) *Social Mobility Delusions: Why So Much of what Politicians Say about Social Mobility in Britain is Wrong, Misleading or Unreliable.* London, Civitas.

Shayer M, Ginsberg D., (2009) *Thirty years on – a large anti-Flynn effect/ (II): 13- and 14-year-olds. Piagetian tests of formal operations norms 1976–2006/7.* British Journal of Educational Psychology, Volume 79, pp. 409-418.

Skinner B.F., (1991) *The behaviour of organisms.* Copley Publishing Group.

Titcombe R., Davies R., (2006) *Curriculum Change and School Improvement. TES.*

Titcombe, R., (2006) *Cognitive Ability and School Improvement.* Practical Research for Education, Issue 36.
[Online] available at:
www.nfer.ac.uk/nfer/PRE_PDF_Files/06_36_06.pdf

Titcombe, R., (2008) *How Academies Threaten the Comprehensive Curriculum.* Forum, 50(1)

Titcombe, R., (2011) *A Case Study in School Improvement.* Forum, 53(3).

Vygotsky, L., (1978) *Mind in Society.* Harvard University Press.

Herbert W., Hollis M, (2000) *Strong Words.* Newcastle: Bloodaxe Books.

Wolf, A., (2011) *Review of Vocational Education,* London: Department for Education.

Wolpert, L., (1993) *The Unnatural Nature of Science.* London: Faber and Faber.

## About the author

Roger Titcombe was an enthusiastic science teacher for thirty-two years, including eleven years in Leicestershire where he became Vice-Principal and Acting Principal of a Leicestershire 14-18 school. He completed an M. Ed (distinction) at Leicester University in 1982 and has maintained a career long interest in the relationship between curriculum and learning. In 1989 he was appointed Headteacher of an inner urban 11-16 school in a northern industrial town from which post he retired in 2003. He has since been an independent educational researcher. He is married with six grandchildren and lives in South Cumbria.

CPSIA information can be obtained at www.ICGtesting.com
Printed in the USA
LVOW10s1500270315

432300LV00003B/342/P